BITTER TO BETTER

"Do You Want To Be Made Well?"

Rev. Dr. Nancy Hulshult

BITTER TO BETTER: "DO YOU WANT TO BE MADE WELL?"

ISBN: 979-8-9856988-7-9

Published by:
Narratus Creative | Narratus Press
P.O. Box 1413
Hamilton, OH 45012

Layout/Design: Narratus Creative | narratuscreative.com
Cover Photo Credits: Evan Hulshult

Produced in the United States of America

FOREWORD

Breathtaking and heart revealing! In this book, *Bitter or Better: "Do You Want To Be Made Well?"* Nancy spells it out so simply: do we really seek for true healing so we can be made whole? Nancy Hulshult captures the true essence of forgiveness and the heart of our Father God calling His people to a place of surrender: surrendering our trauma, our hurts, our bitterness and unforgiveness so we can truly be healed and made whole. Nancy takes us on a loving journey reminding us of the cost Jesus paid for us! Her loving, anointed words radiate off the pages with love and warmth, leading us back to a place of safety and security as we unveil our fears and doubts before the Father God, asking for total forgiveness so we can be free.

This book paints a beautiful portrait of love and displays a roadmap on how to get set free from the roots of bitterness that can so cloud your heart and sway your judgment. Nancy, thank you so much for those quiet moments with God in the pool. Thank you for your listening heart and your yielded spirit to hear the Father's cry concerning His people and His love to see them set free from bitterness and unforgiveness so His people can get better. This book is a must read for those who have struggled, doubted, feared, or even feel bitter because of life's circumstances.

Thank you, Nancy!

Apostle Stacie Johnson B.S, M.A, Ph.D Candidate, LCDCIII
(CEO) **Women of Vision Global Network**

OTHER BOOKS BY NANCY HULSHULT

- *I'm Still Here: From Cold War to COVID, Stories of My Spiritual Journey* (2020)
  - *Aún Sigo Aquí* (Spanish Edition) (2021)

- *Imagine You! 40 Days of Devotions: Finding Your Identity in God's Image* (2021), co-author with Francesca King
  - *¡Imagínate A Ti!: 40 Días de Devociones: Encontrar Tu Identidad a Imagen de Dios* (Spanish Edition) (2021)

- *God's Restorative Nature* (2022), co-author with Chad P. Shepherd

- *The Manna God: 40 Days in Exodus* (2023)

- *Javelin Over Jericho: 24 Principles of Leadership from Joshua* (2023)

DEDICATION & APPRECIATION

Thanks to Darrell Hulshult, for living by Philippians 4:8 as husband, father, grandfather, friend, and servant leader. *"Finally, brothers and sisters, whatever is true, whatever is noble, whatever is right, whatever is pure, whatever is lovely, whatever is admirable—if anything is excellent or praiseworthy—think about such things."*

Thanks to our sons, our daughters-in-love, and our grandchildren, who fuel our lives with love, laughter, tears, purpose, and hope for our next generations.

Thanks to all who have contributed your words that give evidence of the power of the Holy Spirit in the lives of those who call Jesus Christ our Lord and Savior:

Rachel Bane, contributing writer, speaker, author, *The Messy Life*, Host of Podcast *"Wildly Becoming"*;

Denise Chaney, publisher, NarratusCreative, and author, *Unlikely Grace: This Is My Story, This Is My Song: Reflections, Revelations & Honest Questions for the Church I Love*;

Debbie Day, editor and contributing writer;

Apostle Stacie L. Johnson, CEO of Women of Vision Global Network, and author, *An Unveiled Heart, The Sons of Thunder: The Real Truth About Prison Ministry And The Men Behind Bars*;

Gea Jones-Thompson, mission-minded servant leader and contributing writer;

Lena Ramsey Kilgore, former youth pastor and servant leader, for the soul-searching challenge that prompted the writing of this book;

Erin Tunnat Mann, my Goddaughter, contributing writer and speaker;

Rev. Dr. Bonnie Newell, author, *One at a Time: The Life of Roma Lee Courvisier, That'll Preach: Timeless Sermons by Arlo Newell (The 1950's)*, and *Can You?* (Children's Book);

Matt Nicol, Hamilton High School social studies teacher, speaker, and contributing writer; Fellowship of Christian Athletes Advisor; Academic Quiz Team Coach (and publicly proclaimed on Facebook as "Disciple of Christ. Husband. Father. History nerd. In that order");

Erica Williams, contributing writer and Life Coach, Life Coaching & Consulting Associates;

Thanks to Mary Lou Hudek, editor, friend, and member of The Ukeladies;

Thanks to Sheryl Burk, editor and friend;

Thanks to Evan Hulshult, grandson and photographer for book cover.

IN MEMORY OF HAMILTON FIRE CAPTAIN BRANDON A. HUDSON

1976-2023

"A good day is a day somebody doesn't die." — Brandon to a news reporter after escaping death from a fall through the roof of a house on fire on July 4, 2017.

One of the last times that I saw Brandon, he was sitting behind me at church in 2023. I shared with him that I was working on a book about overcoming bitterness. A good storyteller himself, Brandon said that he could tell me lots of stories about bitterness. We set a date and time for him to share, and he came prepared to tell his story in three parts. Part One was "Bitterness Breakthrough in the Family" after his first fire. In addition to the support he received from his brotherhood of firefighters, Brandon said that he leaned on his wife and children for his calming influence. Part Two was "Bitterness Breakthrough in Small Group" after training gone wrong. He said that he had joined a Bible study group and had rededicated his life at the church altar. Part Three was "Bitterness Breakthrough in the Brokenness" after his career as a firefighter ended abruptly due to his injuries. He said that he was "jolted into journaling" and was starting to receive daily Bible verses on his phone to help him focus on scripture.

In reference to his state of mind during our manuscript meeting, Brandon had said, "I have felt more peace and love. The kids see that I am happier. I enjoy walking now. I wanted to do my job, but I am at peace with retiring medically. I want my wife to be happy. If one, or both of us, is bitter, we'll pass bitterness on to our kids. If we are both happy, we will pass happiness on to them. And who doesn't want our children to be happy? Life is hard; I don't need to make it any harder."

Brandon died before we reached the point of publishing his chapter for this book. As much as we all try, not all of us are able to survive bitterness, anger, disappointment, and grief, but we must try for our own sake and for the sake of our family and friends. Brandon's funeral was a packed church with firefighters, family, and friends who consider him a hero. May his life be remembered for his service toward others and his love for Jesus.

TABLE OF CONTENTS

INTRODUCTION

¹After this there was a feast of the Jews, and Jesus went up to Jerusalem. ²Now there is in Jerusalem by the Sheep Gate a pool, which is called in Hebrew, Bethesda, having five porches. ³ In these lay a great multitude of sick people, blind, lame, paralyzed, waiting for the moving of the water. ⁴For an angel went down at a certain time into the pool and stirred up the water; then whoever stepped in first, after the stirring of the water, was made well of whatever disease he had. ⁵Now a certain man was there who had an infirmity thirty-eight years. ⁶When Jesus saw him lying there, and knew that he already had been in that condition a long time, He said to him, "Do you want to be made well?"

⁷ he sick man answered Him, "Sir, I have no man to put me into the pool when the water is stirred up; but while I am coming, another steps down before me."

⁸Jesus said to him, "Rise, take up your bed and walk." ⁹ And immediately the man was made well, took up his bed, and walked. —John 5:1-9 (NKJV)

Jesus' question to the paralyzed man may have sounded peculiar. What sick person wouldn't want to be made well? Perhaps some people do not want their situations to change. After 38 years in a state of paralysis, maybe the man was resigned to live the rest of his life that way. For those of us today who have been bitter about life's circumstances, perhaps we are content to live the rest of our lives bitter, complaining, wallowing in our discontent. Consider folks who do nothing but retell how life has been difficult or folks who love to recount who mistreated them and how they have been miserable since then. Maybe bitterness is so ingrained in their spirits that they don't know that they have a choice to release the bitter spirit. Truly it is a choice to let go of bitterness and become well, whole, content.

Think of Jesus asking you today, "Do you want to be made well?" Or perhaps, "Do you want to become better and let go of bitterness?"

The sick man answered Jesus by saying that he has no one to help him to get into the healing waters. Jesus directs him to rise, take up his bed, and walk. That sounds simple. Just get up and walk away! But in the man's mind, this action was inconceivable because he had never been able to make it as far as the pool.

Perhaps you would answer Jesus like this: "I want to feel better but I don't know how." Or "I don't have anyone to help me." Remove the "I" in your thinking. If you are choosing to be made well, then this book will help you to know how, and you will read about others and how they were made well. Make the choice to let go of "bitter" and become "better". Stop thinking about how much "I" have been hurt or disappointed. Just one small adjustment in your life can lead to a "better" sense of wholeness and positive mindset toward others. Rather, choose the "e" in "she", "he", or "they", or perhaps how you want "to be": BETTER!

For fun, think of solving a word puzzle, like the TV game show, Wheel of Fortune. Contestants compete for money and prizes by successfully filling in the blanks of words or phrases. They take turns spinning the wheel with different cash values and choose one letter at a time. So far Vanna White has uncovered the consonants, showing you "B _ T T _ R." Is the answer "butter"? "batter"? "bitter"? Or "better"? You can choose to "buy a vowel", and the difference between winning and losing is one correct letter. Viewers at home are watching and cheering for you, hoping that your next choice will be "e"! You make that choice and become the winner. You get your amassed cash and prizes, and life for you just became a bit better! Congratulations!

In Jesus' name, I pray that you choose better over bitter today. "Do you want to be made well? Rise. Take up your bed and walk." I suggest that you leave behind the bed of bitterness that you have made and have wallowed in for a long time. Just rise and walk. Move forward with your life in wholeness and health. Choose good health of your mind and a strong sense of humility in your spirit.

DEFINITIONS OF BITTER AND BETTER:
Definition of bitter: (of people or their feelings or behavior) angry, hurt, or resentful because of one's bad experiences or a sense of unjust treatment.

Definition of better: partly or fully recovered from illness, injury, or mental stress; less unwell.

I talk to God while I swim laps for an hour each weekday. I start by praising the Lord and thanking God for my many blessings. Before or after I "speak" to say what is in my heart or on my mind, I stay quiet in the cool waters and listen. Sometimes I feel the Lord talking, and sometimes flashes of visions show me what the Holy Spirit wants to teach me. Here is the one that prompted me to write this book.

THE VISION OF THE VASE

Behold a terra cotta vase that was formed and fired by the potter's hand. It served its purpose of holding flowers for display. One day it was smashed to the ground, the water spilled out, and the flowers wilted. The once beautiful and functional vase was indistinguishable in its pile of shards and dust. Gently and methodically, the potter picked up each broken piece and joined it to another with putty and glue. Patiently designing the sharp edges and angled curves, the potter fashioned the most gorgeous piece of mosaic art. The potter then added white caulk and a glaze that reflected different colors when placed in the sun. Behold this new work of art, whose purpose is the appreciation of the potter. It is a reminder that what the enemy tried to destroy, the potter raised up and restored to greater strength and beauty.

When I asked the Holy Spirit what this meant for me, I heard, "Do not dwell on your former image or the past, and do not put a hammer in someone else's hands."

When I went home to my devotional space, I sought scripture for more wisdom.

> *For God, who said, "Let light shine out of darkness," made his light shine in our hearts to give us the light of the knowledge of God's glory displayed in the face of Christ. But we have this treasure in jars of clay to show that this all-surpassing power is from God and not from us. We are hard pressed on every side, but not crushed; perplexed, but not in despair; persecuted, but not abandoned; struck down, but not destroyed."* —2 Corinthians 4:6-9

I would like to say that I have moved on from all past traumas, but at times I have been stuck in bitterness when something, someone, or some thought carries me right back to the point of deep hurt and disappointment. I had practiced the biblical mandate from Jesus to forgive others "not seven times, but seventy-seven times":

> "Then Peter came to Jesus and asked, "Lord, how many times shall I forgive my brother or sister who sins against me? Up to seven times?" Jesus answered, "I tell you, not seven times, but seventy-seven times."—Matthew 18:21-22

I found that the mental exercise of my mind had not eliminated the emotions in my heart. Might the emotions always remain in my heart but without a bitter reaction? Is it possible to eliminate emotions associated with experiences?

With love and forgiveness in his heart, Jesus proclaimed from the cross,

> "Father, forgive them for they know not what they do." —Luke 23:34

With residual bitterness and hurt in my heart, my prayers sounded more like this: "Lord, you told me that I have to forgive the jerk(s) who knew exactly what they were doing when they hurt me, so I will." I can see the face of the resurrected Jesus wincing and saying, "That is not exactly what I had in mind for you to have peace in your life." We are called to forgive and to love. The first letter of John spells out clearly that we are not merely called to forgive and to love, but we are commanded to do so.

> "For this is the message you heard from the beginning: We should love one another. Do not be like Cain, who belonged to the evil one and murdered his brother. And why did he murder him? Because his own actions were evil and his brother's were righteous. Do not be surprised, my brothers and sisters, if the world hates you. We know that we have passed from death to life, because we love each other. Anyone who does not love remains in death. Anyone who hates a brother or sister is a murderer, and you know that no murderer has eternal life residing in him.
>
> This is how we know what love is: Jesus Christ laid down his life for us. And we ought to lay down our lives for our brothers and

sisters. If anyone has material possessions and sees a brother or sister in need but has no pity on them, how can the love of God be in that person? Dear children, let us not love with words or speech but with actions and in truth.

This is how we know that we belong to the truth and how we set our hearts at rest in his presence: If our hearts condemn us, we know that God is greater than our hearts, and he knows everything. Dear friends, if our hearts do not condemn us, we have confidence before God and receive from him anything we ask, because we keep his commands and do what pleases him. And this is his command: to believe in the name of his Son, Jesus Christ, and to love one another as he commanded us. The one who keeps God's commands lives in him, and he in them. And this is how we know that he lives in us: We know it by the Spirit he gave us". —1 John 3:11-24

Moving beyond forgiveness to love our transgressors is not easy, particularly if the hurt is deep and repetitive. To truly love another is to forgive to the point of praying blessings over them and asking God for salvation and freedom for you and them. It is more in my nature to forgive and try to forget than it is to forgive and remember to pray for my transgressors. That is my challenge.

For hurts that are impossible to forget, the challenge is to choose healthy and helpful responses that do not allow the hurt to continue or to deepen. That is part of the purpose of this book. Dwelling on hurts from the past only continues the painful emotions. Asking why I was the victim (rather than anyone else) leads to a sense of helplessness, anger, guilt, or low self esteem. It is the difference between a wound that has become a faint scar and a scab that we continue to pick so that it stays oozy and infected. I can look at a faint scar and acknowledge that I was hurt, but now I am (almost) as good as new. If I don't let the wound heal, I am in constant pain or discomfort, which affects my peace of mind and restoration of my soul.

In talking with a friend one day, she challenged me on whether or not I had completely forgiven a person that had caused me great distress and changed the trajectory of my life. My words said "yes" but my tone and non-verbal expressions revealed that I still had not completely moved on from my pain. How do I move forward and stop the spiraling thoughts and emotions that would take me right back to the root cause of my hurt? I continued to ask God for help. As I prayed, image after image came to my mind, and I hurriedly jotted down a title for each one. Every image came with specific strategies and details, which came to be known as "My 30 Brainstorming Bitterness Busters" in Chapter 5.

Then another friend sent me a verse from Scripture that helped me further.

> *"Don't expect anyone else to fully understand both the bitterness and the joys of all you experience in your life."* —Proverbs 14:10 TPT

Exactly. None of us can fully understand the bitter and joyful times in our own lives. If you are hanging on to bitterness, let's work through our struggles together.

Before I share the strategies that God gave to me during my prayer time, let's look closely at four people from Scripture who turned their bitterness into joy: Esau, Joseph, Naomi, and David. Each of their stories shows some form of bitterness and disappointment within their family. We can all relate to struggles within family relationships and loss, which makes these four people excellent resources from which to draw lessons in overcoming bitterness. Besides being faithful to God and family, what did they do in order to live more joyful lives?

PSALM 86:5
You, Lord, are forgiving and good,
abounding in love to all who call to you.

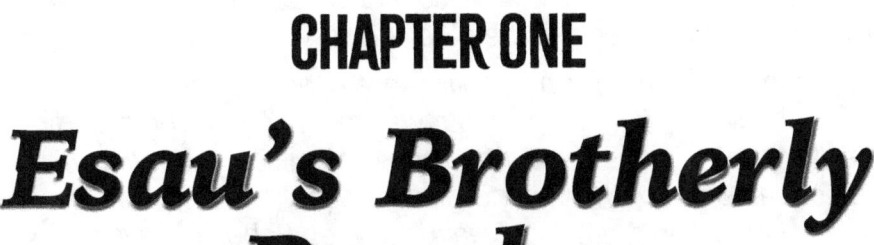

CHAPTER ONE

Esau's Brotherly Resolve

BITTER TO BETTER

Consider Esau, who had the greatest reason to stay angry and bitter towards his father, Isaac, and his twin brother, Jacob. Younger brother, Jacob, had been literally tugging at his older brother's heel since birth and continued to lie and deceive their father in order for Jacob to earn Esau's birthright and their father's blessing. The account is detailed in the book of Genesis.

> Isaac prayed to the Lord on behalf of his wife, because she was childless. The Lord answered his prayer, and his wife Rebekah became pregnant. The babies jostled each other within her, and she said, "Why is this happening to me?" So she went to inquire of the Lord.
>
> The Lord said to her, "Two nations are in your womb, and two peoples from within you will be separated; one people will be stronger than the other, and the older will serve the younger."
>
> When the time came for her to give birth, there were twin boys in her womb. The first to come out was red, and his whole body was like a hairy garment; so they named him Esau. After this, his brother came out, with his hand grasping Esau's heel; so he was named Jacob. Isaac was sixty years old when Rebekah gave birth to them. — Genesis 25:21-26

Even though they were twins, Esau and Jacob looked different and possessed different skills and interests. While in today's world, we often say that parents should not show favoritism among their children, Scripture says that their mother favored Jacob, and their father favored Esau.

> The boys grew up, and Esau became a skillful hunter, a man of the open country, while Jacob was content to stay at home among the tents. Isaac, who had a taste for wild game, loved Esau, but Rebekah loved Jacob. —Genesis 25:27-28

Scripture goes on to say that Esau came home from hunting starving so much so that he sold his birthright as the oldest son to Jacob for some bread and lentil stew. Apparently Esau was so hungry that he felt close to death, so his birthright would have been meaningless to him, had he died from starvation. Rebekah concocted a scheme for Jacob to steal Esau's birthright from him by having Jacob dress up like Esau and cook a meal for his father as requested of Esau. While

Esau was out hunting game for the meal, Jacob cooked a home grown meal of a couple of young goats from their own flocks. Father Isaac fell for the ruse and transferred the birthright and blessing to Jacob, much to Esau's dismay.

If ever there were a bitter brother, it was Esau. His mother and twin brother plotted against him, his father gave away his birthright and blessing, and he was denied the pleasure of his father eating the delicious last meal that he had hunted and prepared for him.

Here is the father's blessing that Esau should have received but was lost to his brother Jacob:

> *"Ah, the smell of my son is like the smell of a field that the Lord has blessed. May God give you heaven's dew and earth's richness— an abundance of grain and new wine. May nations serve you and people bow down to you. Be lord over your brothers, and may the sons of your mother bow down to you. May those who curse you be cursed and those who bless you be blessed."*
> — Genesis 27:27-29

Here is the father's blessing that Esau received as a "second blessing", per Esau's request:

> *His father Isaac answered him, "Your dwelling will be away from the earth's richness, away from the dew of heaven above. You will live by the sword and you will serve your brother. But when you grow restless, you will throw his yoke from off your neck."*
> —Genesis 27:39-40

Once the blessing left his mouth, Isaac would not recant the blessing. The promise, the blessing, the birthright, all the favor of the oldest son was permanently transferred to the younger son. No wonder Esau's grudge grew to the point of wanting to kill his brother. Instead of the earth's richness, Esau was promised a dwelling away from the earth's richness. Instead of heaven's dew, Esau was promised a dwelling away from heaven's dew. Instead of being lord over his brothers, Esau was promised that he would live by the sword and serve his brother.

How was this fair? (How often do we hear our children ask the same question of their parents when they have made decisions regarding fair treatment among their siblings?)

BITTER TO BETTER

Consider the following exchange between Esau and father Isaac. Esau desperately asks his father for any type of blessing that might have been reserved for him. The only positive part of the "second blessing" is hope for a time when Esau will be free from Jacob's "yoke" from his neck.

> *Isaac trembled violently and said, "Who was it, then, that hunted game and brought it to me? I ate it just before you came and I blessed him—and indeed he will be blessed!" When Esau heard his father's words, he burst out with a loud and bitter cry and said to his father, "Bless me—me too, my father!" But he said, "Your brother came deceitfully and took your blessing."*
>
> *Esau said, "Isn't he rightly named Jacob? This is the second time he has taken advantage of me: He took my birthright, and now he's taken my blessing!" Then he asked, "Haven't you reserved any blessing for me?"*
>
> *Isaac answered Esau, "I have made him lord over you and have made all his relatives his servants, and I have sustained him with grain and new wine. So what can I possibly do for you, my son?"*
>
> *Esau said to his father, "Do you have only one blessing, my father? Bless me too, my father!" Then Esau wept aloud.*
>
> *His father Isaac answered him, "Your dwelling will be away from the earth's richness, away from the dew of heaven above. You will live by the sword and you will serve your brother. But when you grow restless, you will throw his yoke from off your neck."*
>
> *Esau held a grudge against Jacob because of the blessing his father had given him. He said to himself, "The days of mourning for my father are near; then I will kill my brother Jacob."*
> — Genesis 27:33-41

Esau maintained respect for his dying father and planned to mourn him, but then he turned his anger and bitterness toward his brother with intent to kill him.

Fearful of losing both sons, Rebekah sent Jacob off and told him that he could return when his brother was no longer angry and forgot what happened.

Let's pause and let Rebekah's words sink in so that we can feel the anger and bitterness of Esau at a deeply personal level to see how we might respond.

> *When Rebekah was told what her older son Esau had said, she sent for her younger son Jacob and said to him, "Your brother Esau is planning to avenge himself by killing you. Now then, my son, do what I say: Flee at once to my brother Laban in Haran. Stay with him for a while until your brother's fury subsides. When your brother is no longer angry with you and forgets what you did to him, I'll send word for you to come back from there. Why should I lose both of you in one day?"*— Genesis 27:42-45

Who of us would forget how we were deceived, betrayed, and robbed of what was due to us from birth? Who of us could no longer be angry about our mother and brother teaming up against us and treating our father like an old fool, who couldn't tell the difference between his sons' voices, smell, and touch, or the difference between a home grown meal of young goats and the taste of wild game? As deceived as Isaac was, he maintained the integrity of his blessing and would not recant it. What a dysfunctional family, right? Does this sound similar to any dysfunctional families today?

How would Esau ever get over his anger and bitterness toward his family, especially his twin brother, Jacob? Scripture shows us how Esau responds and resolves his anger and bitterness.

In Genesis 26:34-35, Esau married two women who were a source of grief to his parents.

> *When Esau was forty years old, he married Judith daughter of Beeri the Hittite, and also Basemath daughter of Elon the Hittite. They were a source of grief to Isaac and Rebekah.* — Genesis 26:34-35

Scripture does not provide details about Esau's intentions to gain his parents' approval through his choices to marry Hittite (Canaanite) women, but verse 26:35 is clear that they were a source of grief to them. After being denied his birthright, we may think that Esau may have not cared whether or not they were pleased with his choices of having married outside of the Abrahamic covenant. However, after hearing Isaac tell Jacob not to marry Canaanite women, Esau takes steps to gain his parents' approval by marrying a woman from the tribe of Ishmael. Once again, however bitter Esau was against Jacob, his actions show that he wanted to remain in his father's graces.

Disgusted with Esau's wives, Rebekah took steps to protect her favorite son, Jacob, by sending him away to marry someone from Harran where her brother Laban lived.

> Then Rebekah said to Isaac, "I'm disgusted with living because of these Hittite women. If Jacob takes a wife from among the women of this land, from Hittite women like these, my life will not be worth living." — Genesis 27:46

Then Isaac prayed another blessing over Jacob before he left for Haran:

> "May God Almighty bless you and make you fruitful and increase your numbers until you become a community of peoples. May he give you and your descendants the blessing given to Abraham, so that you may take possession of the land where you now reside as a foreigner, the land God gave to Abraham."— Genesis 28:3-4

This blessing must have been difficult for Esau to hear after being cheated out of his birthright and blessing. For a second time, his father blesses Jacob with fruitfulness of people and of land, the land given to Abraham. Jacob's blessing guarantees him a part of the promise given to Abraham by God.

Interestingly, in the following verses, Esau realized his father's displeasure of the Canaanite wives. No mention is made here of any concern for his mother's displeasure or disapproval.

> Now Esau learned that Isaac had blessed Jacob and had sent him to Paddan Aram to take a wife from there, and that when he blessed him he commanded him, "Do not marry a Canaanite woman," and that Jacob had obeyed his father and mother and had gone to Paddan Aram. Esau then realized how displeasing the Canaanite women were to his father Isaac; so he went to Ishmael and married Mahalath, the sister of Nebaioth and daughter of Ishmael son of Abraham, in addition to the wives he already had.
> —Genesis 28:6-9

By Chapter 32, there had been no resolution between Jacob and Esau, as documented here. Jacob knew that he needed to return, but he was still afraid of Esau.

Jacob sent messengers ahead of him to his brother Esau in the land of Seir, the country of Edom. He instructed them: "This is what you are to say to my lord Esau: 'Your servant Jacob says, I have been staying with Laban and have remained there till now. I have cattle and donkeys, sheep and goats, male and female servants. Now I am sending this message to my lord, that I may find favor in your eyes.'"

When the messengers returned to Jacob, they said, "We went to your brother Esau, and now he is coming to meet you, and four hundred men are with him."

In great fear and distress Jacob divided the people who were with him into two groups, and the flocks and herds and camels as well. He thought, "If Esau comes and attacks one group, the group that is left may escape."

Then Jacob prayed, "O God of my father Abraham, God of my father Isaac, Lord, you who said to me, 'Go back to your country and your relatives, and I will make you prosper,' I am unworthy of all the kindness and faithfulness you have shown your servant. I had only my staff when I crossed this Jordan, but now I have become two camps. Save me, I pray, from the hand of my brother Esau, for I am afraid he will come and attack me, and also the mothers with their children. But you have said, 'I will surely make you prosper and will make your descendants like the sand of the sea, which cannot be counted.'"

He spent the night there, and from what he had with him he selected a gift for his brother Esau: two hundred female goats and twenty male goats, two hundred ewes and twenty rams, thirty female camels with their young, forty cows and ten bulls, and twenty female donkeys and ten male donkeys. He put them in the care of his servants, each herd by itself, and said to his servants, "Go ahead of me, and keep some space between the herds."

He instructed the one in the lead: "When my brother Esau meets you and asks, 'Who do you belong to, and where are you going, and who owns all these animals in front of you?' then you are to say, 'They belong to your servant Jacob. They are a gift sent to my lord Esau, and he is coming behind us.'"

He also instructed the second, the third and all the others who followed the herds: "You are to say the same thing to Esau when you meet him. And be sure to say, 'Your servant Jacob is coming behind us.'" For he thought, "I will pacify him with these gifts I am sending on ahead; later, when I see him, perhaps he will receive me." So Jacob's gifts went on ahead of him, but he himself spent the night in the camp. — Genesis 32:3-21

Jacob had remained fearful of his twin brother, Esau, through all the years that he had grown to own many livestock and two camps of people. As he prepared to return home, Jacob knew that he would have to make peace with Esau or die trying. He was not sure of Esau's present state of mind. He just knew that Esau was coming toward him with 400 men.

In Chapter 33, Jacob sent all of his gifts ahead of him to Esau, including all the women and children in order to soften Esau's heart (and to guard himself.) Then he went ahead and bowed down to the ground seven times as Esau approached him.

Jacob looked up and there was Esau, coming with his four hundred men; so he divided the children among Leah, Rachel and the two female servants. He put the female servants and their children in front, Leah and her children next, and Rachel and Joseph in the rear. He himself went on ahead and bowed down to the ground seven times as he approached his brother. — Genesis 33:1-3

In the next verses, Esau ran to meet his brother and hugged and kissed him, and they cried together. Then Esau asked Jacob to introduce his family to him.

But Esau ran to meet Jacob and embraced him; he threw his arms around his neck and kissed him. And they wept. Then Esau looked up and saw the women and children. "Who are these with you?" he asked.

Jacob answered, "They are the children God has graciously given your servant."

Then the female servants and their children approached and bowed down. Next, Leah and her children came and bowed down. Last of all came Joseph and Rachel, and they too bowed down. — Genesis 33:4-7

Esau accepted Jacob's gifts after Jacob insisted, and Esau offered to accompany Jacob to his destination.

Esau asked, "What's the meaning of all these flocks and herds I met?"

"To find favor in your eyes, my lord," he said.

But Esau said, "I already have plenty, my brother. Keep what you have for yourself."

"No, please!" said Jacob. "If I have found favor in your eyes, accept this gift from me. For to see your face is like seeing the face of God, now that you have received me favorably. 11 Please accept the present that was brought to you, for God has been gracious to me and I have all I need." And because Jacob insisted, Esau accepted it.

Then Esau said, "Let us be on our way; I'll accompany you." — Genesis 33:8-12

When Jacob declined Esau's generous offer of accompaniment, Esau then offered protection to Jacob and his family. Esau continued to offer grace to his brother. Esau must have turned from all thoughts and feelings of bitterness, because for Jacob, his brother's face was like seeing the face of God. Everything about Esau reflected God's grace and love. He was transformed from the time when he had first parted ways with his brother in anger and bitterness. Now he was truly freed from the brother's yoke that his father Isaac had spoken about in his blessing:

"You will live by the sword and you will serve your brother. But when you grow restless, you will throw his yoke from off your neck." — Genesis 27:40

Esau had replaced the yoke around his neck with an embrace around his brother's neck. Finally he was free of the anger and bitterness that had choked him. Wouldn't it be wonderful to see the face of God in the face of the person to whom we are asking forgiveness? To receive grace from another is to receive grace from God.

Genesis 35 tells of a beautiful restored relationship of the brothers with the account of their father's death.

> *Jacob came home to his father Isaac in Mamre, near Kiriath Arba (that is, Hebron), where Abraham and Isaac had stayed. Isaac lived a hundred and eighty years. Then he breathed his last and died and was gathered to his people, old and full of years. And his sons Esau and Jacob buried him.* — Genesis 35:27 -29 (NKJV)

There is much more written about Jacob and his Abrahamic descendants. However, this account of Esau's life shows the possibilities of reconciliation from the most extreme conflicts in a family. We read of Esau, the son stripped of everything that was promised to him; Esau, the brother bitter to the point of wanting to murder his deceiving twin; Esau, the husband, who married to the disappointment of his mother and then for the approval of his father; Esau, the strong man who used his strength and skills to build a camp of more than 400 men, land, and livestock; and Esau, the faithful follower of God, who worked through his disappointments in life to forgive his brother of all past transgressions.

ESAU'S 10 DECISIONS FOR A (BITTER) FREE LIFE

The following 10 lessons from Esau help us to battle bitterness:

1. Esau continued to respect his parents.
   If you are seeking a bitter free life, respect your parents, even when you do not agree with their decisions.

2. Esau learned what his parents valued and acted accordingly (marriage with the Abrahamic family line).
   If you are seeking a bitter free life, learn and understand the values of your parents and make intentional decisions to accept or reject those values for your future family according to the truth from the Word of God.

3. Esau exercised self-control by not acting on his first emotions of anger and violence.

> *If you are seeking a bitter free life, exercise self-control by not harming others in the wake of your anger or disappointment.*

4. Esau regrouped and made his own way by living by the sword, as was spoken over him by his father.

   > *If you are seeking a bitter free life, overcome past hurts by resetting your present and future in healthy ways spiritually, mentally, and physically.*

5. Esau learned to serve, as was spoken over him by his father.

   > *If you are seeking a bitter free life, learn how to serve others rather than serving yourself through self-pity or other negative emotions.*

6. With grace, Esau responded to his brother's gestures toward reconciliation by coming to meet Jacob.

   > *If you are seeking a bitter free life, stay open to reconciliation from others who have hurt you, if they are repentant and safe, and extend them grace.*

7. With grace, Esau didn't wait for his brother to reach him; he ran to embrace and kiss his brother.

   > *If you are seeking a bitter free life, take the first step toward reconciliation, even if you were the victim of past hurts, if your transgressor is repentant and safe.*

8. With grace, Esau extended his forgiveness to his brothers' family, asking about Jacob's women and children.

   > *If you are seeking a bitter free life, extend forgiveness to anyone who may have been a part of a past hurt unknowingly or unintentionally.*

9. With grace, Esau offered to come alongside his brother to accompany him on his journey.

   > *If you are seeking a bitter free life, offer to help someone who has hurt you, as much as possible, if he or she is repentant and safe.*

10. With grace, Esau offered protection to his brother.

   > *If you are seeking a bitter free life, be reconciled with a past repentant transgressor to the point of partnership, as much as possible.*

BITTER TO BETTER

Esau is the consummate bitterness buster! Instead of living with bitterness, Esau became a man of great grace. He had fought through his anger, disappointment, and betrayal as he continued to value and respect his parents and family. It could not have been easy to let go of his birthright that had been promised to him since Jacob grabbed his heel in the womb. However, he managed to be fruitful and prosperous in new ways by using his God given skills and talents. Jacob could steal Esau's birthright and blessing through outward deceptions, but no one could rob Esau of all for which God had equipped him for his future.

Before we move on to look at the life of Joseph, let's talk about birthrights, inheritances, and modern day issues over "the will." Most folks will say that parents or grandparents, or anyone, for that matter, have the right to decide what happens to their earthly possessions. Legally, they establish a will that is shared before or after their death. However, their attempts to be fair, wise and just are often questioned by the living recipients.

Bitterness, disappointment, anger, resentment, jealousy, greed, and a whole list of unholy emotions fester and lead to an entire family being divided over the spoils left behind. Entire families have been fractured or completely torn apart over inheritances. A once loving group of siblings can turn into a civil war over "stuff". It is not uncommon today. Esau and Jacob were not the only children fussing over inheritances. Have you heard any of the following discussions among family members or friends' families? How were the issues resolved? Peacefully, I hope!

- One child had borrowed money from the parents. Should the debt be factored into each person's "fair share"?

- One child took care of the parents until death, while another child took off and traveled the world, never looking back. Should they each get equal shares?

- Should biological children and step-children be given equal shares?

- One child was hateful to the parents, wrecked the family car, stole money from them, and caused heartache for years. The other children were kind and helpful. Should they be given equal shares of the inheritance?

- The children are struggling financially and were expecting thousands of dollars in inheritance but learned that their parents gave most of their money to charity. Should they contest the will?

- One child fell on hard times, and the other fell into wealth, should they both receive equal shares?

- The children received equal shares of the money, but one child swooped in and took all of the antiques and collectibles from their parents' home, saying that the items were gifts given before their death. Should the items be returned or divided? If so, how?

- One child has special needs, and the other children do not. Does the special needs child deserve to have a larger portion of the inheritance?

- Every child owns a house, except for one. Should that child get the parents' house, or should they sell the house and divide the profits from the sale?

- What happens to the family car? Does it go to a new driver or the child driving a junker? Does it get sold and the profits divided evenly?

If you are in a Jacob and Esau conflict, what can you do to make peace within your family? Can there be healthy conversations about inheritances and wills while all parties are still alive to talk about the decisions being made? Would it be helpful to understand the circumstances of all parties involved, or would it be wise to trust the parents to disburse their wealth in the way that they fit? Are you prepared to learn that your parents plan to give all their money and possessions to charity instead of to their children or grandchildren? Clarification and understandings, even if all do not agree, would be helpful in the process of wills and inheritances. Don't be bitter. Be better!

Psalm 130:3-5
If you, Lord, kept a record of sins,
* Lord, who could stand?*
But with you there is forgiveness,
* so that we can, with reverence, serve you.*
I wait for the Lord, my whole being waits,
* and in his word I put my hope.*

CHAPTER TWO

Joseph's Journey to Wholeness

BITTER TO BETTER

Joseph's story begins with him as the favored baby brother, who gets treated unkindly and suffers abuse and near death at the hands of his jealous brothers.

> *Now Israel loved Joseph more than any of his other sons, because he had been born to him in his old age; and he made an ornate robe for him. When his brothers saw that their father loved him more than any of them, they hated him and could not speak a kind word to him.* — Genesis 37:3-4 (TPT)

As the youngest child sent by his father to check on the older brothers, Joseph brought back a bad report to the father. In addition, Joseph dreamed prophetic dreams, including dreams that his brothers would bow down to him, and shared them with his brothers, which escalated their bitterness and jealousy toward him. The brothers strip Joseph of his ornate robe and throw him in an empty cistern in the wilderness. They sell Joseph to passing Ishmaelites (Midianite merchants) and spill animal blood on the robe to lie to their father about the whereabouts of the favored son. The Midianites sold Joseph to Potiphar in Egypt.

In Genesis 38, Joseph lived in Potiphar's house and was put in charge of the entire household. When Potiphar's wife made advances toward Joseph, he refused and escaped, but he couldn't escape the false accusations and was imprisoned. In prison, Joseph found favor with the warden and was put in charge again.

In Genesis 39, Joseph interpreted dreams accurately for Pharaoh's chief cupbearer and chief baker when they were imprisoned together. The baker was executed, as prophesied through his dream, and the cupbearer was restored to his position, also as prophesied through the dream. The chief cupbearer promised Joseph to put in a good word for him to Pharaoh, but he forgot him until no one but Joseph could interpret Pharaoh's dream. As a result, Joseph was put in charge of Egypt.

Between the ages of 17 and 30, Joseph found favor with those with authority over him; he forgave his family; and he was able to cast off any bitterness about his mistreatment by his brothers, Pharaoh, and the chief cupbearer. He had taken his focus from his woes and turned his focus to being fruitful and productive in his service and in his family.

Before the years of famine came, two sons were born to Joseph by Asenath, daughter of Potiphera, priest of On. Joseph named his firstborn Manasseh and said, "It is because God has made me forget all my trouble and all my father's household." The second son he named Ephraim and said, "It is because God has made me fruitful in the land of my suffering." —Genesis 41:50-52

In Genesis 45, Joseph expresses his love for his brothers and father and his lack of bitterness toward any of them.

Then Joseph said to his brothers, "Come close to me." When they had done so, he said, "I am your brother Joseph, the one you sold into Egypt! And now, do not be distressed and do not be angry with yourselves for selling me here, because it was to save lives that God sent me ahead of you. For two years now there has been famine in the land, and for the next five years there will be no plowing and reaping. But God sent me ahead of you to preserve for you a remnant on earth and to save your lives by a great deliverance.

"So then, it was not you who sent me here, but God. He made me father to Pharaoh, lord of his entire household and ruler of all Egypt. Now hurry back to my father and say to him, 'This is what your son Joseph says: God has made me lord of all Egypt. Come down to me; don't delay. You shall live in the region of Goshen and be near me—you, your children and grandchildren, your flocks and herds, and all you have. I will provide for you there, because five years of famine are still to come. Otherwise you and your household and all who belong to you will become destitute.' — Genesis 45:4-11

Even though Joseph had been mistreated and put in the most difficult of situations, he continued his faithfulness to God, his dreaming prophetic dreams, his ability to interpret the dreams, and his ability to lead with skill and love for people. Bitterness could not take control of Joseph's heart or mind. He considered every step of his journey to be from God for God's purpose. Seeing the world through the lens of God's love and purposes for us will help us to relinquish any bitterness that we have harbored from people who have mistreated us.

No one more adequately expresses how Joseph overcame bitterness than his father, Jacob, praying his last blessing over his sons. Jacob describes Joseph as the prince among his brothers. Even though Joseph's attackers were bitter toward him, he remained steady, strong, and faithful to the Mighty One, the Shepherd, the Rock of Israel, the God who helps and blesses:

> *"Joseph is a fruitful vine, a fruitful vine near a spring, whose branches climb over a wall.*
>
> *With bitterness archers attacked him; they shot at him with hostility.*
>
> *But his bow remained steady, his strong arms stayed limber, because of the hand of the Mighty One of Jacob, because of the Shepherd, the Rock of Israel,*
>
> *because of your father's God, who helps you, because of the Almighty, who blesses you with blessings of the skies above, blessings of the deep springs below, blessings of the breast and womb.*
>
> *Your father's blessings are greater than the blessings of the ancient mountains, than the bounty of the age-old hills. Let all these rest on the head of Joseph, on the brow of the prince among his brothers."* —**Genesis 49 :22-26**

JOSEPH'S 10 DECISIONS TOWARD A (BITTER) FREE LIFE

Consider the following ten decisions that helped Joseph to break through bitterness:

1. Joseph remained faithful to his father. As a young man, he brought back reports about his brothers to his father, as requested of him. When he gained authority over his brothers in Egypt, Joseph brought his father to Egypt and cared for him.
    If you are seeking to break through bitterness, refrain from having a vindictive spirit and show a caring spirit to others, even members of your family.

2. Joseph remained faithful to his heavenly father, praising God for his fruitfulness and blessings.
    If you are seeking to break through bitterness, remain faithful to God and notice His interventions in your life.

3. Joseph told the truth, even when the truth was not what people wanted to hear, especially his dreams about his brothers and

Pharaoh's dreams about the upcoming famine.

If you are seeking to break through bitterness, tell the truth, even when the truth is unpopular or may cause you harm.

4. Joseph used his God-given gifts to help others, even in his dire circumstances. He interpreted dreams for those around him.

   If you are seeking to break through bitterness, tap into your God-given talents to help others, thereby focusing on the positive impact you will have on others.

5. Joseph remained pure in heart, mind, and body. When Potiphar's wife tempted him, he did not hesitate to escape the temptation.

   If you are seeking to break through bitterness, remain pure in heart, mind, and body.

6. Joseph looked forward in hope for a better future, even through setbacks. When the king's cupbearer forgot about acknowledging him to Pharaoh, Joseph did not lose heart.

   If you are seeking to break through bitterness, look forward in hope, even through setbacks.

7. Joseph made connections with other people. No matter where he was, he connected with other people, which resulted in better circumstances for himself.

   If you are seeking to break through bitterness, continue to make positive connections with positive people who can help you.

8. Joseph cared for people beyond himself and his own family. After interpreting Pharaoh's prophetic dream about future famine, Joseph used his wisdom and authority to store up food for all of Egypt.

   If you are seeking to break through bitterness, find ways to impact the world beyond yourself and your immediate family. Make a difference!

9. Joseph trusted in God's purpose for his life and did not hold a grudge against his brothers for betraying him. He saw God using all that happened to him as a benefit to him.

   If you are seeking to break through bitterness, trust in God's purpose for your life and do not hold grudges that will hold you back from spiritual growth.

10. Joseph forgave his transgressors. In the beginning of his hardship, Joseph thanked God for helping him to forget his troubles and his father's household. Then his brothers came to him asking for help in the famine. He was unable to forget them or their sin against him because they were standing right in front of him. He had to make the decision to forgive them or punish them. After hosting his brothers (incognito) and giving himself time to adjust to the return of his brothers to his presence, Joseph was able to forgive and to care for his family.

If you are seeking to break through bitterness, forgive your transgressors. Forgiveness is as healthy for you as it is for the remorseful transgressor. If your transgressor is not remorseful, forgive anyway and relieve yourself of the burden.

Psalm 55:22

Cast your cares on the Lord
and he will sustain you;
he will never let
the righteous be shaken.

CHAPTER THREE

"Can this be Naomi?"

BITTER TO BETTER

Naomi was a woman from Bethlehem who was blessed with a husband and two sons. Because of a famine, their family moved to Moab, but there her husband and sons died. Only her two daughters-in-law remained, and Naomi wanted to send them back to their people for a chance to marry and have a better life. Orpah went back to her own family, but Ruth vowed to stay with Naomi.

When Naomi and Ruth received word that the famine had lifted, they decided to return to Bethlehem. Apparently their return caused a stir in the small town with the women asking the question, "Can this be Naomi?"

> *So the two women went on until they came to Bethlehem. When they arrived in Bethlehem, the whole town was stirred because of them, and the women exclaimed, "Can this be Naomi?"*
>
> *"Don't call me Naomi," she told them. "Call me Mara, because the Almighty has made my life very bitter. I went away full, but the Lord has brought me back empty. Why call me Naomi? The Lord has afflicted me; the Almighty has brought misfortune upon me."*
> —Ruth 1:19-21

This is an Interesting question, considering that we can't read the tone of the question. Did they ask, "Can this be Naomi?" because of their surprise, because she was not traveling with her husband, or because her countenance had changed so much since her days in Bethlehem?

Whatever the women may have been thinking and saying aloud about her physical appearance, Ruth clarified exactly how she was feeling. She was bitter, so bitter that she rejected her name Naomi, which means "pleasant" or "lovely", and asked to be called Mara, which means "bitter". In other places in the Bible, name changes occur when God has moved in miraculous ways, such as Abram being renamed Abraham by God, or Simon being renamed Peter by Jesus. In Naomi's case, she renames herself because she is so distraught that God has afflicted her with such misfortune. Not only was she grieving the death of her husband and two sons, she would be grieving the loss of potential grandchildren and her own situation of being a widow in a patriarchal society. Many reasons caused her to be bitter and to proclaim her bitterness to the women of Bethlehem, and she blamed God, the Almighty.

When Ruth finds food by gleaning Boaz's field, Naomi expresses appreciation, even as she calls herself "the dead."

"The Lord bless him!" Naomi said to her daughter-in-law. "He has not stopped showing his kindness to the living and the dead. "She added, "That man is our close relative; he is one of our guardian-redeemers." — Ruth 2:20

Naomi showed love and concern for others as she worked through her bitterness, beginning with Ruth.

Naomi said to Ruth, her daughter-in-law, "It will be good for you, my daughter, to go with the women who work for him, because in someone else's field you might be harmed." — Ruth 2:22

Naomi tapped into her positive experiences from the past as a loving wife to guide Ruth through her relationship and courtship with Boaz.

One day Ruth's mother-in-law Naomi said to her, "My daughter, I must find a home for you, where you will be well provided for. Now Boaz, with whose women you have worked, is a relative of ours. Tonight he will be winnowing barley on the threshing floor. Wash, put on perfume, and get dressed in your best clothes. Then go down to the threshing floor, but don't let him know you are there until he has finished eating and drinking. When he lies down, note the place where he is lying. Then go and uncover his feet and lie down. He will tell you what to do."

"I will do whatever you say," Ruth answered. So she went down to the threshing floor and did everything her mother-in-law told her to do. —Ruth 3:3-6

Naomi moved on from her past by selling her deceased husband's property through Boaz. She did not dwell on her bitter emotions but made the decision in order for Ruth to have security.

Boaz took ten of the elders of the town and said, "Sit here," and they did so. Then he said to the guardian-redeemer, "Naomi, who has come back from Moab, is selling the piece of land that belonged to our relative Elimelek. I thought I should bring the matter to your attention and suggest that you buy it in the presence of these seated here and in the presence of the elders of my people. If you will redeem it, do so. But if you will not, tell me, so I will know. For no one has the right to do it except you, and I am next in line."

"I will redeem it," he said.

Then Boaz said, "On the day you buy the land from Naomi, you also acquire Ruth the Moabite, the dead man's widow, in order to maintain the name of the dead with his property."

At this, the guardian-redeemer said, "Then I cannot redeem it because I might endanger my own estate. You redeem it yourself. I cannot do it." — Ruth 4:2-6

Naomi released her bitterness in a show of receiving God's love and restoration by taking the baby in her arms and caring for him.

So Boaz took Ruth and she became his wife. When he made love to her, the Lord enabled her to conceive, and she gave birth to a son. The women said to Naomi: "Praise be to the Lord, who this day has not left you without a guardian-redeemer. May he become famous throughout Israel! He will renew your life and sustain you in your old age. For your daughter-in-law, who loves you and who is better to you than seven sons, has given him birth." Then Naomi took the child in her arms and cared for him. The women living there said, "Naomi has a son!" And they named him Obed. He was the father of Jesse, the father of David. — Ruth 4:13-17

By the end of the book of Ruth, we see Naomi holding a newborn baby and women pronouncing, "Naomi has a son!" Biologically, the baby is not her son or grandson, since Naomi was only related to Ruth through marriage. However, because Boaz had purchased Naomi's property from her kinsman-redeemer, baby Obed now serves as her guardian-redeemer. Because of Naomi's decisions and actions from her grief to Obed's birth, her "son" becomes the father of Jesse, father of David, and through the Messianic lineage to Jesus, the Redeemer.

How did Naomi bust through her bitterness toward God to her praise to Him for her guardian-redeemer? Naomi took action. She moved. She decided to return to her homeland when she heard that the Lord had provided food for her people in Judah.

NAOMI'S 7 DECISIONS TOWARD A (BITTER) FREE LIFE

Consider the following eight decisions that Naomi made to cope with her grief:

1. Naomi took an assessment of her current reality. She decided or realized that she was too old to marry and have sons who could marry her daughters-in-law, so she wanted them to return to their people for a better life.

   Decide to live a bitter free life by being honest with yourself and assessing your current state of mind and circumstances. Do I really want to continue living in constant grief?

2. Naomi did not stay isolated. Despite insisting that the daughters-in-law return home, Naomi accepted help from her daughter-in-law, Ruth, who promised to be by her side wherever she would go.

   Decide to live a bitter free life by accepting help from others and being part of a community, no matter how big or small.

3. Naomi was thankful for God's provision. Even through her bitterness, when Ruth finds food by gleaning Boaz's field, Naomi expresses appreciation, even as she calls herself "the dead."

   Decide to live a bitter free life by being thankful to God for provision in whatever form the blessings may come.

4. Naomi showed love and concern for others as she worked through her bitterness, beginning with Ruth.

   Decide to live a bitter free life by showing love and concern for others, even as you work through your bitterness or grief.

5. Naomi tapped into her positive experiences from the past as a loving wife to guide Ruth through her relationship and courtship with Boaz.

   Decide to live a bitter free life by tapping into your positive experiences from the past and applying them to your present circumstances, where applicable.

6. Naomi moved on from her past by selling her deceased husband's property through Boaz. She did not dwell on her bitter emotions but made the decision in order for Ruth to have security.

   Decide to live a bitter free life by not clinging to the past and by making decisions toward health and security.

7. Naomi released her bitterness in a show of receiving God's love
   and restoration by taking the baby in her arms and caring for him.
   Decide to live a bitter free life by showing love to others
   unconditionally. Hospital volunteers in the Neuro Intensive
   Care Unit (NICU) will testify to the warm feelings that they get
   in return from loving the littlest in need. Help those who can't
   help themselves.

1 John 2:9–10

*"Whoever loves his brother
abides in the light,
and in him there is no
cause for stumbling."*

CHAPTER FOUR

David's Overcoming Bitterness Not "One and Done"

While writing about breaking through bitterness, I have spoken with many friends and writers about this topic. With every conversation come new thoughts, ideas, and considerations. My friend and editor, Debbie Day, talked about situations where a person could experience bitterness caused by another person, not just one time, but over and over again. Debbie brought such a rich perspective to our conversation that I asked her to record her thoughts and allow me to include them in this book. She consented, and here is her take on the topic of bitterness as seen in the lives of David and Saul from Scripture.

"DAVID DID IT"

Overcoming bitterness toward a person or situation is possible, but what do we do when repeated transgressions are inflicted on us by the same person? A person may face various stages of overcoming bitterness caused by someone's words or actions. Saul sought after David to kill him because he was jealous of the success and popularity of David. Instead of feeling animosity toward Saul, David allowed God to work on his heart as he actually fled for his life. We can see this change happening in David's heart when David had the opportunity to kill Saul; instead, he just cut off a piece of Saul's robe to show him that he did not take that opportunity. Even after that, David felt guilty because he said that he was not giving respect to God's anointed. Dealing with hurt and trying to do the right thing can be difficult. Although Saul cried and seemed to repent, acknowledging the good David had done and asking David to take care of his descendants, his change of heart was short-lived.

Once again Saul made plans to kill David because Saul's hate and jealousy was stirred up. Again David happened upon Saul; this time Saul was sleeping. David had repented of wanting to retaliate against Saul, but now David was in a similar situation. Our enemy, the devil, does not give up easily. Just because we resisted once does not mean we will resist temptation again. But David did resist again. As Saul lay sleeping with his spear and water jug beside him, David could have easily killed Saul. Instead, David took the weapon and the water and was able to show them to Saul as he stood on a hill across a canyon. Saul repented again. Because he was under attack by the Philistines, Saul did not try to kill David again.

Although David did not want to kill Saul, he still did not completely trust him and knew that Saul was not going to be successful in battle because he had stopped trusting God. This situation is similar to what we face when we see someone who has hurt us deeply facing difficulties of his/her own. David did not delight in Saul's failures. When he heard of the death of Saul and his sons, including Jonathan, who David loved dearly, David lamented, "Oh how the mighty have fallen... " (2 Samuel 1:19). David was truly heartbroken, even though this meant that he would now be king. We see that later David kept his promise to Saul and found the remaining descendents of Saul and took care of them.

It is not easy to stop feeling bitterness toward those who hurt and anger us, especially when it continues to happen. It takes much prayer and vigilance to continue to allow God to work on our hearts and to dig out roots of bitterness. Negative thoughts and desires easily become negative comments and actions if we allow the roots of bitterness a chance to grow. If David can forgive Saul for the evil he did to him, we know that God can help us overcome what we perceive to be injuries to us brought on by others.

DAVID'S 5 DECISIONS TOWARD A (BITTER) FREE LIFE

1. David chose to flee rather than to fight when Saul sought to kill David.

    Choosing forgiveness, like David, sometimes requires us to walk away or avoid a fight that would make relationships worse.

2. Even when Saul was in error, David continued to show respect because Saul was God's anointed.

    Choosing forgiveness, like David, requires that we forgive with love and respect for our transgressors.

3. David was put in a position to retaliate or forgive more than once concerning the same transgressor, Saul.

    Choosing forgiveness, like David, sometimes requires that we forgive the same transgressor more than once.

4. David did not delight in Saul's failures, even when Saul's death meant that David would become king.

Choosing forgiveness, like David, requires that we refrain from delighting in the failures of our transgressor.

5. David continued to forgive Saul, but he did not continue to trust him.

    Choosing forgiveness, like David, does not necessarily mean that we choose to trust our transgressor.

John 10:10

*"The thief comes only
    to steal and kill and destroy;
I have come that they
    may have life,
and have it to the full."*

CHAPTER FIVE

30 Brainstorming Bitterness Busters

WHAT THE NEW TESTAMENT WRITERS SAY ABOUT BITTERNESS

And do not grieve the Holy Spirit of God, with whom you were sealed for the day of redemption. Get rid of all bitterness, rage and anger, brawling and slander, along with every form of malice. Be kind and compassionate to one another, forgiving each other, just as in Christ God forgave you." — Ephesians 4:30-32

Make every effort to live in peace with everyone and to be holy; without holiness no one will see the Lord. See to it that no one falls short of the grace of God and that no bitter root grows up to cause trouble and defile many. See that no one is sexually immoral, or is godless like Esau, who for a single meal sold his inheritance rights as the oldest son. — Hebrews 12:14-16

Who is wise and understanding among you? Let them show it by their good life, by deeds done in the humility that comes from wisdom. But if you harbor bitter envy and selfish ambition in your hearts, do not boast about it or deny the truth. Such "wisdom" does not come down from heaven but is earthly, unspiritual, demonic. —James 3:13-15

MY RECENT LESSONS ABOUT OVERCOMING BITTERNESS

I don't know how deep your bitterness goes, nor do I know the extent of joy that you have felt in life, but I pray that all of us experience much more joy than bitterness. Causes of bitterness or joy come into our lives that we may not be able to control, but we can affect the extent that we are affected by these emotions. We can choose to dwell on joy and to diminish bitterness by how we control our thoughts and actions.

We need to weigh the cost of bitterness and disappointment. Allow me to relate a simple story from my trip to the gas pump today. I pulled my car into the gas station, inserted my rewards card, and read on the screen this question, "Would you like to receive .06 off per gallon today?" Why, yes I would! I hit the "yes" button and proceeded to insert my credit card, removed it, and began filling my gas tank. I noticed that the price of the gas had not changed from the original price, so I checked my receipt. Nope. No savings at all was reflected on the receipt. I pulled around to the front door of the store and took my receipt, credit card, and rewards card in hand. I related my disappointment to the employee at the register, to which she responded, "Oh, no, you don't get .06/per gallon off today. That sale went off two days ago. It just hasn't been changed at the pump."

"But I didn't get any cents off, not .03, not .06. I paid full price. Can you refund me the difference, even if it's just the .03/gallon savings?"

"No, I can't, and besides, you already put the gas in your car."

I asked to speak to the manager, and another employee handed me a consumer relations comment card with a phone number. "You can complain here."

"OK. Thank you."

"I'm sorry."

It was nice just to have someone apologize for my distress, but as I put my hand on the door to leave, the first employee said, "Have a nice rest of your day!" Before the door had closed, I heard the two employees cackling, and I had been the only one in the store. I started to fume.

I sat in the parking lot of the gas station and called the consumer relations number and left a voicemail. When I got home, still fuming, I wrote a followup email to make sure that my complaint was registered with the company.

As I typed at my computer, I realized that I had been upset over losing $1.20 in savings. For the cost of a candy bar, I had made myself angry, disgusted, bitter, and aggravated for two hours. Two hours of my life had been wasted because of a computerized gas pump and one young impertinent cashier. I thought of all the wonderful, loving thoughts and ideas that could have filled my mind for two hours! Instead I chose all the negative reactions. I told myself that I was never going back to that store, that I would demand recompense from the company, and that I should go to social media and tell all my (less than 100) Facebook friends not to go to that store. I was so wrong! I let a small, unexpected disappointment turn me into a bitter, cranky old woman, probably deserving of a chuckle from my dramatic upset at the register.

I did better at the grocery store, where the cashier and the bagger stopped to admire my purchases. "Hey, look! They sell spaghetti sauce called 'Yo Mama's!'" "Oh, that chocolate silk pie looks yummy!" Yes, I was in a hurry, but no, I didn't say a word. Well, I did glance behind me to see two other customers waiting with full grocery carts. At least I was almost checked out and on my way. It could be worse.

This book is specifically about busting the bitterness that lurks in our hearts and bubbles to the surface when we least expect it or when we allow it. As in the opening story of the vase turned to the colorful mosaic, we can allow the Lord to redesign ourselves from brokenness to beauty. Try one or more of the following 30 ideas and see if they help you to bust your bitterness. Turn your mourning into dancing, your bitterness to joy. Let your thoughts work in sync with your heart for complete healing. If none of these 30 ideas resonate with you, hold on and be inspired by the amazing testimonies that follow!

30 BRAINSTORMERS TO BUST BITTERNESS
by Nancy Hulshult

1. THE "ESCAPE ROOM"
Think of yourself being trapped in bitterness with no apparent way to escape. You know that there is a way out, but you must search for clues that lead you step by step out of the trap and into freedom. There are several clues that come to my mind, but you may find others specifically catching your eye. Test and see if they lead you closer to where you want to be. Picture all of the following in your Escape Room and try any one or all of these strategies:

- A slip of paper with scripture for wisdom
- A telephone to call a close friend for encouragement (not gossip)
- A prayer card with words for healing in Jesus' name
- A musical instrument and a praise song to God
- A thank you card to write to God for all your blessings
- A photo of your favorite family member who loves you unconditionally
- A piece of hard candy to suck on (no crunching) for reducing anger or anxiety

- A piece of paper and pen to write a letter of encouragement to yourself
- A calendar with list of things to do that help other people
- An invitation to your own pity party limited to one hour per week, no guests allowed
- A piece of fruit for sweet sensations
- A vegetable for healthier living
- A key that comes with forgiveness for others and for yourself

With their mouths the godless destroy their neighbors, but through knowledge the righteous escape. — Proverbs 11:9

2. REVERSE BINOCULARS

Instead of focusing on the source of your bitterness and magnifying it until it seems larger than life, try imagining looking through the opposite side of the binoculars. Whatever or whoever caused you to focus on your bitterness and enlarge your situation will now look much, much smaller and insignificant. Perhaps you are not ready to "unsee" it, but you are in a better place than you were before.

So we fix our eyes not on what is seen, but on what is unseen, since what is seen is temporary, but what is unseen is eternal.
—2 Corinthians 4:18

3. REHEARSE FOR THE NEXT PERFORMANCE

Search, study, and memorize scriptures that help you to understand, forgive, and speak love and peace to others. When Jesus was tempted by Satan on the mountaintop, Jesus used scripture to stop any temptation and to defeat Satan with God's Word. You can do that, too. Be ready for any potential pop-up encounter with your source of bitterness. It is not if it will happen; it is when it will happen. Let Scripture guard your heart...and mouth.

Then Jesus was led by the Spirit into the wilderness to be tempted by the devil. After fasting forty days and forty nights, he was hungry. The tempter came to him and said, "If you are the Son of God, tell these stones to become bread."

Jesus answered, "It is written: 'Man shall not live on bread alone, but on every word that comes from the mouth of God.'"

Then the devil took him to the holy city and had him stand on the highest point of the temple. "If you are the Son of God," he said, "throw yourself down. For it is written: "'He will command his angels concerning you, and they will lift you up in their hands, so that you will not strike your foot against a stone.'"

Jesus answered him, "It is also written: 'Do not put the Lord your God to the test.'"

Again, the devil took him to a very high mountain and showed him all the kingdoms of the world and their splendor. "All this I will give you," he said, "if you will bow down and worship me."

Jesus said to him, "Away from me, Satan! For it is written: 'Worship the Lord your God, and serve him only.'"

Then the devil left him, and angels came and attended him.
—Matthew 4:1-11

4. STRIP DOWN TO THE REAL YOU

If you are carrying bitterness around with you day and night, try this exercise. Dress in as many layers of clothing as possible. With each layer, say aloud what is making you angry, bitter, resentful, or regretful. Then walk around the house or do a little exercise to feel the full weight of the clothing. After an hour or so, stand before your mirror and look at yourself loaded down with all those layers that come from a heavy heart. With each layer that you remove, say to yourself as you look in the mirror, "I am no longer going to wear bitterness." With the next layer, "I am no longer going to wear anger." And so on.... When you get down to the last layer, go ahead! Take it all off and see yourself as God made you, promising yourself and God that you will only put on the garment of salvation and the robe of righteousness (Isaiah 61:10). As you get dressed each day, remember or say aloud, "Lord, I live this day wearing my garment of salvation and robe of righteousness. Let me no longer put on anything else that would weigh me down or keep me from feeling love and peace."

"Don't shed any blood. Throw him into this cistern here in the

wilderness, but don't lay a hand on him." Reuben said this to rescue him from them and take him back to his father.

So when Joseph came to his brothers, they stripped him of his robe—the ornate robe he was wearing— and they took him and threw him into the cistern. The cistern was empty; there was no water in it. —Genesis 37:22-24

5. CIRCLE YOUR WAGONS

This is an old expression from the Wild West when settlers would circle their wagons to defend themselves from attacks. By making a circle, they made themselves less vulnerable to their enemies and able to support each other from a position of solidarity. To bust through bitterness, form a circle of solid support made up of your closest friends and family whom you trust. Then when you feel under attack, you have people who can help you regroup and buffer that bitterness that always seems to return when you least expect it.

"I will set a sign among them, and I will send some of those who survive to the nations—to Tarshish, to the Libyans and Lydians (famous as archers), to Tubal and Greece, and to the distant islands that have not heard of my fame or seen my glory. They will proclaim my glory among the nations. And they will bring all your people, from all the nations, to my holy mountain in Jerusalem as an offering to the Lord—on horses, in chariots and wagons, and on mules and camels," says the Lord. "They will bring them, as the Israelites bring their grain offerings, to the temple of the Lord in ceremonially clean vessels. And I will select some of them also to be priests and Levites," says the Lord.— Isaiah 66:19-21

6. BE A CLOWN!

The song lyrics go, "Be a clown! Be a clown! All the world loves a clown..." It's hard not to smile when a silly happy clown looks at you with those big eyes, red nose, and wide painted smile. In the same way, it's hard not to frown when a sad clown with teary eyes looks at you; you find yourself frowning as well. This may work in real life as well. Smile! It may be difficult when you are fighting bitterness, but smile anyway. In your mind, when you go about your day, think of yourself as a happy clown out to make others smile. You'll find yourself smiling more, and eventually you will be smiling inside more.

BITTER TO BETTER

If your imagination is not working with this idea, then do it! Sit in front of your mirror and paint your face into a happy clown. Make faces at yourself. Take selfies of you clowning around. Then try your biggest frown. It will look silly, too.

Win with a grin.
Go miles with smiles.
Smiling automatically makes people look more attractive.

What's to lose? Only your bitterness and anger. Now come on. Show me that smile!

> *"People listened to me expectantly,*
>   *waiting in silence for my counsel.*
> *After I had spoken, they spoke no more;*
>   *my words fell gently on their ears.*
> *They waited for me as for showers*
>   *and drank in my words as the spring rain.*
> *When I smiled at them, they scarcely believed it;*
>   *the light of my face was precious to them.*
> *I chose the way for them and sat as their chief;*
>   *I dwelt as a king among his troops;*
>   *I was like one who comforts mourners.* —Job 29:21-25

7. FEED YOUR SOUL, NOT YOUR EMOTIONS THROUGH YOUR STOMACH

Guilty! I'm so guilty of feeding my emotions. Whether I'm really happy or really sad or really mad or really hurt, my hands reach for the refrigerator as I stand with the doors open ready to devour all my favorite treats. When I'm particularly angry, crunchy potato chips and Cheetos help me to grind my angry teeth together while tasting the saltiness of disappointing people or situations.

Try managing your emotions by foregoing the fats and sugars that will make you heavy and grumpy the next day. Instead, try feeding your soul by reading a good book or listening to an audio book. The Bible, a devotional, Christian fiction, or any uplifting story that encourages you will help you to reduce bitterness and anger. You may find yourself refocusing on the positive sides of life.

> *He humbled you, causing you to hunger and then feeding you*
> *with manna, which neither you nor your ancestors had known,*

to teach you that man does not live on bread alone but on every word that comes from the mouth of the Lord.
— Deuteronomy 8:3

8. TAKE A POTTERY CLASS OR LESSON

Spend some time with your hands in wet clay as you become a potter and make something new (and possibly even indescribable!) As your hands move and the wheel turns, you may feel your heart soften and your bitterness turn to joy, even if the result is a glob of mud that you title "My Former Self."

Yet you, Lord, are our Father. We are the clay, you are the potter; we are all the work of your hand. — Isaiah 64:8

9. BE YOUR OWN BARISTA OR CHEF

Work out your bitterness by creating a better you! Keep fruits, veggies, and yogurt on hand to make a delicious smoothie. Expand your skills in making soothing lattes and espressos. Work your way to creating an in-house salad bar by cutting, chopping and grating all the best ingredients to keep you healthy. Not only will your food look appetizing, the energy expended on the prep will work off negative emotions that you didn't know you still had.

Then God said, "I give you every seed-bearing plant on the face of the whole earth and every tree that has fruit with seed in it. They will be yours for food. — Genesis 1:29

10. TRADE PING PONG FOR TENNIS

If you can't resist the bitter game of life that urges you to have a reaction to every irritating "ping" that comes your way with a "pong" comment, slam, or text, stop playing! While seemingly impossible, you can actually stop an argument by refusing to reply. You can actually stop bitterness by refusing to churn the gossip wheel with others. You can actually stop the revolving thoughts in your mind by switching games, like switching to tennis.

In tennis, you get two chances to "serve", you "rally" when you go back and forth, and even when your score is zero, it's called "love." Awww....see? How we think about things is affected by semantics, by the words we use to describe.

BITTER TO BETTER

Put a stop to ping ponging with your bitterness and think about life as serving, rallying, and love.

> *If I speak in the tongues of men or of angels, but do not have love, I am only a resounding gong or a clanging cymbal. If I have the gift of prophecy and can fathom all mysteries and all knowledge, and if I have a faith that can move mountains, but do not have love, I am nothing. If I give all I possess to the poor and give over my body to hardship that I may boast, but do not have love, I gain nothing.*
> — 1 Corinthians 13:1-3

11. THE CUTTING ROOM FLOOR

The "cutting room floor" is a term used for any unused or scrapped footage not included in the finished version of a film. It could also be pages deleted from the original manuscript that didn't make it to the final printing of a book. Think about your bitter thoughts, feelings, and actions that affect the best days of your life. Choose to reimagine the story of your life without them, thus leaving them on the cutting room floor. You don't need them, and nobody else does either.

In your mind, see yourself trimming your daily life to only include the best of what God has and wants for you.

Every day is a new day. Every day is an opportunity for a clean start. Wake up. Walk into a new day grateful and looking forward to the newness of what God has in store for you!

> *You will surely forget your trouble, recalling it only as waters gone by. Life will be brighter than noonday, and darkness will become like morning.* — Job 11:16-17

12. DELETE YOUR REPLAY/REWIND BUTTON OR TURN THE CHANNEL

Unless you need evidence in a court of law, there is no need to replay times in your life when bitterness crept in. You lived it; now leave it. Bitterness is not fodder for a joyful, godly life; it is the fertilizer that comes from the wrong end of a farm animal. Let it pass! Turn off the bitter channel of thoughts in your brain and flip to a better channel of positive thoughts.

If you are tempted to press rewind, try the fast forward button instead, and see what life lies ahead for you when walking in love, serving others, and sharing the gospel of peace wherever you go. Guaranteed you will sleep better at night and face each day with a more positive attitude.

But in keeping with his promise we are looking forward to a new heaven and a new earth, where righteousness dwells.
— 2 Peter 3:13

13. JOIN WITH POSITIVE PEOPLE

Don't isolate yourself in your bitter misery. Leave it behind and join a group of Christian people who love unconditionally and live life unapologetically sold out for Jesus. Find a small group for Bible study; a social group that does things together, like serving or playing sports; or a prayer group who truly prays and refrains from making a gossip list instead of a list of concerns. If not church, then join a YMCA for exercise, a quilting group, a weight lifting team, or a walking club. Make sure that you are around others, at least some of the time, and not solely confined to your own habits, routines, and thoughts. Solitary confinement does not help battle bitterness. Well, unless you want to join a monastery, which would curb your temptation to flap your bitter lips of disappointment.

Every day they continued to meet together in the temple courts. They broke bread in their homes and ate together with glad and sincere hearts, praising God and enjoying the favor of all the people. And the Lord added to their number daily those who were being saved. — Acts 2:46-47

14. WALK IT OFF

Many sports coaches have tried to get an injured player back in the game by telling the player to "walk it off". The player regroups from the injury, if possible, by getting up, stretching out, and walking around for a bit until the pain subsides. This is not always effective, but there is merit to walking to reduce anxiety, anger, and bitterness. Walking regularly has the benefits of better breathing, stronger muscles, and improved mental health. Whether walking alone or walking with one or more friends, reduce your emotional burden by "walking it off" on a regular basis.

Follow God's example, therefore, as dearly loved children 2 and walk in the way of love, just as Christ loved us and gave himself up for us as a fragrant offering and sacrifice to God. But among you there must not be even a hint of sexual immorality, or of any kind of impurity, or of greed, because these are improper for God's holy people. — Ephesians 5:1-3

15. TALK IT OUT

As long as you are not repeatedly dwelling on your bitterness, talk your feelings out with someone who has empathy and who is a good listener. Even if the listener doesn't say a word, or maybe nods a few times as you process your thoughts or experiences, you will feel better by unloading your mind and heart and releasing emotional pain and bitterness into the air. Picture yourself with a balloon inside your chest that fills with air every time you think of your pain, disappointment, heartache, or bitterness. Your balloon eventually stretches bigger and bigger until you can barely breathe from all the pent up emotions. Let it out! Breathe! Talk it out. If you don't, your balloon will burst, and your body will feel the negative effects of harboring all of the burdens without a release. One way or another, your pain will find its way to the surface. You will be able to better control the outcome if you take measures to let it out gradually and peacefully.

"You can see for yourselves, and so can my brother Benjamin, that it is really I who am speaking to you. Tell my father about all the honor accorded me in Egypt and about everything you have seen. And bring my father down here quickly."

Then he threw his arms around his brother Benjamin and wept, and Benjamin embraced him, weeping. And he kissed all his brothers and wept over them. Afterward his brothers talked with him. — Genesis 45:12-15

16. SPIT IT OUT

People may refer to a disappointment or humiliation or something unpleasant as having to "swallow a bitter pill". Don't do it! Don't swallow that pill of bitterness. Spit it out. Remember the warnings about the red dye in maraschino cherries? True or false, I was cautious enough with the artificially colored fruit to stop ingesting them. The same goes for anything related to bitterness. Be cautious about consuming the bitterness and allowing it to affect your body, your energy level, your heart rate, and whatever else is affected by negative emotions. Spit that bitter pill farther than a watermelon seed! You don't need it. You don't want it. Now spit…just not on anyone else. They don't need your bitter germs, either.

> *There some people brought to him a man who was deaf and could hardly talk, and they begged Jesus to place his hand on him. After he took him aside, away from the crowd, Jesus put his fingers into the man's ears. Then he spit and touched the man's tongue. He looked up to heaven and with a deep sigh said to him, "Ephphatha!" (which means "Be opened!").* — Mark 7:32-34

17. DANCE IT OFF

Some religious denominations disapprove of dancing, but David danced before the Lord, and so can you. You don't have to go to a nightclub to dance off your bitterness and negative emotions. You can dance at a YMCA in a zumba class, but you won't be able to choose your music. Instead, dance at home in your living room when no one is watching, choose your Christian music, and get your praise dance on! Dance with grace, dance by jumping and leaping, or dance however the music moves you, and your body will eliminate any pent up anxiousness, anger, bitterness, or lethargy. Move. Just move. Don't worry about what you look like. No one is watching. Focus on the lyrics or melody of the song, and praise God through your dancing.

There is a radio station, 93.3, that plays the same song every Monday morning: Crowder's "I Saw The Light" that moves into "I'll Fly Away" to a country banjo-picking rhythm. The radio announcers use it as a mood lifter. The rhythm and words instantly make the listeners smile, clap, or dance around. Typically on a Monday morning, I'm driving in my car and find myself singing along and slapping my leg, almost dancing in my seat. "I saw the light. I saw the light. No more darkness. No more night. Now I'm so happy. Praise the Lord. I saw the light." No matter how many times I hear this song, my response is the same. I feel happier by the end of the song. Give it a try, or create your own "dance off" at home!

There is a time for everything, and a season for every activity under the heavens:

>   *a time to be born and a time to die,*
>   *a time to plant and a time to uproot,*
>   *a time to kill and a time to heal,*
>   *a time to tear down and a time to build,*
>   *a time to weep and a time to laugh,*
>   *a time to mourn and a time to dance,*
>   *a time to scatter stones and a time to gather them,*
>   *a time to embrace and a time to refrain from embracing,*
>   *a time to search and a time to give up,*
>   *a time to keep and a time to throw away,*
>   *a time to tear and a time to mend,*
>   *a time to be silent and a time to speak,*
>   *a time to love and a time to hate,*
>   *a time for war and a time for peace.*

— Ecclesiastes 3:1-8

18. PUNCH IT OUT

No, don't punch people. It may hurt them and you. Instead, put on the boxing gloves and punch away at the punching bag. Wear yourself out punching the bag that represents your source of bitterness or your pain. When you are worn out physically, you will be less likely to carry the pain out of the exercise room with you. If you still feel residual bitterness, return to the punching bag the next day and have another go at it. You're no Mohammed Ali, but you'll feel like saying, "I'm the greatest, even before I knew I was." Ali also said, "Silence is golden when you can't think of a good answer." And, "It isn't the mountains that wear you down. It's the pebble in your shoe." And one more, "Impossible is just a word thrown around by small men who find it easier to live in the world they've been given than to explore the power they have to change it. Impossible is not a fact. It's an opinion. Impossible is potential. Impossible is temporary. Impossible is nothing."

I must follow Ali's quotes with two from Scripture.

Jesus looked at them and said, "With man this is impossible, but not with God; all things are possible with God." — Mark 10:27

"I have told you these things, so that in me you may have peace. In this world you will have trouble. But take heart! I have overcome the world." — John 16:33

19. PRAY IT OUT

If you want to silence those voices in your mind that keep repeating your bitter moments of life, go to prayer. Every. Time. For me, silent prayer is my usual mode, but when the voices are speaking against my joy and my love for people, then I pray aloud, and louder, if necessary. You can find a prayer space in your home, outside your home, or in your car. If the negative voices compete with your prayers to God, then verbally rebuke the Enemy, or Satan, and say aloud, "I speak to anyone or anything that is not of God, get out of my head. Get out of my space. Get out of my house, in the name of Jesus." And the devil will flee.

Submit yourselves, then, to God. Resist the devil, and he will flee from you.— James 4:7

Here is an expanded version of the same verse from The Message:

So let God work his will in you. Yell a loud no to the Devil and watch him make himself scarce. Say a quiet yes to God and he'll be there in no time. Quit dabbling in sin. Purify your inner life. Quit playing the field. Hit bottom, and cry your eyes out. The fun and games are over. Get serious, really serious. Get down on your knees before the Master; it's the only way you'll get on your feet.
— James 4:7-10 (The Message)

20. FLICK IT

One aversion-therapy technique is the use of a rubber band on the wrist, whereby the wearers snap or flick the rubber band every time they feel stressed. Supposedly, your brain subconsciously avoids the stimulus (stress) to prevent the unpleasant feeling of the snap of the rubber band. People use this technique to try to stop smoking, prevent self-harm, and other like behaviors. If you want to stop the repeated feelings of bitterness or anger, give your rubber band a snap to remind yourself that you are choosing to avoid thinking about past bitterness. Snap and move on. Just flick it.

Suddenly an angel of the Lord appeared and a light shone in the cell. He struck Peter on the side and woke him up. "Quick, get up!" he said, and the chains fell off Peter's wrists. — Acts 12:7

21. WRITE IT DOWN, BURN IT, SOAK IT, DROP IT, AND LET IT GO!

Try writing all your feelings of bitterness and anger on paper. Let it all out. Say what you've always wanted to say to a person or about a situation. Give details. Use as many exclamation points as you wish. Write in caps. Use bold print. Etch the tip of your pen or pencil well into the parchment or paper until it almost tears. Scribble. Sketch a picture of your pain. Whatever is in your head and heart, pour it out on the page. Say what you want to do. Fight back with the most disrespectful words. Don't worry about hurting anyone's feelings or causing any harm, because immediately after you get it all out on paper, burn it in a campfire or some safe way, or soak it in a sink or bucket full of water until all the words and paper are dissolved. When you have destroyed the evidence of your tirade, you should feel calmer and maybe relieved. Then whenever your feelings of bitterness start to return, remind yourself that they have been burned or drowned. They no longer exist. You have let them go. If necessary, repeat and rinse.

Then get over yourself. Pride and carnality prevent us from the fullness of the Holy Spirit in our hearts. We may hang on to bitterness because we wallow in our pride and the flesh because we stay focused on ourselves, thinking, "How dare someone disrespect me? I deserve better than that kind of treatment." Putting aside pride, we realize that we are sinners and imperfect beings who deserve nothing and no special treatment, but God has granted us his mercy and grace to call us his own. Jesus, as the perfect Son of God, deserved all the best but received the worst treatment to death on a cross, yet he put aside pride and his divinity for the salvation of his transgressors and all of us who have sinned against God and our fellow humans.

> The religion scholars and Pharisees led in a woman who had been caught in an act of adultery. They stood her in plain sight of everyone and said, "Teacher, this woman was caught red-handed in the act of adultery. Moses, in the Law, gives orders to stone such persons. What do you say?" They were trying to trap him into saying something incriminating so they could bring charges against him.
>
> Jesus bent down and wrote with his finger in the dirt. They kept

at him, badgering him. He straightened up and said, "The sinless one among you, go first: Throw the stone." Bending down again, he wrote some more in the dirt.

Hearing that, they walked away, one after another, beginning with the oldest. The woman was left alone. Jesus stood up and spoke to her. "Woman, where are they? Does no one condemn you?"

"No one, Master."

"Neither do I," said Jesus. "Go on your way. From now on, don't sin." — John 8:3-11 (The Message)

Interestingly, Scripture notes that the oldest in the crowd walked away first. Why do you suppose the oldest in the crowd would have walked away first? Maybe they had more wisdom that comes with age, or maybe they had longer memories of the many sins from their past (or present) lives. We all need to drop our stones of criticism and judgment of others and choose Jesus, the Rock of our salvation.

22. LAUNCH A BALLOON OF BITTERNESS

Some people launch helium balloons to remember a loved one or to express their grief. As the balloon soars into the sky, the people think of their loved one going to heaven or their sadness being lifted. This can work for bitterness as well. Fill a balloon with helium, or buy one at the dollar store. Spend a few moments speaking your bitterness over the balloon, or writing the words "bitterness" or "anger" or "disappointment" on the balloon. After a prayer to God about your intentions to turn your focus away from yourself and onto the Lord, let the balloon go. Watch it rise higher and higher into the sky. Once it has disappeared, imagine that all your negative emotions have been taken up into the heavens and put into God's hands.

Cast all your worries (or cares or anxiety) upon him, for he cares for you. — 1 Peter 5:7

23. SKIP A ROCK, SINK A WORRY

Choose a rock or several rocks to represent your bitterness, anger, or anxiety. Then, if you want to go a step further, write the word "bitterness" or "anger" or "anxiety" on a rock or several rocks. Stand or sit by a river, creek, or lake and pray about your need to rid yourself of the heaviness that comes from these emotions. When you are ready, skip the rocks far across the water, or throw them as far as you can and watch them sink deep into the water to rest somewhere where you can never go back and pick them up again. When you are tempted to revisit those times of negativity, tell yourself that they are far away and into the deep, never to be recovered again.

He is the Rock, his works are perfect, and all his ways are just. A faithful God who does no wrong, upright and just is he.
— Deuteronomy 32:4

24. LIGHTEN YOUR LUGGAGE

Write the words "bitterness, anger, anxiety, worry, depression...." or whatever you are carrying around on separate pieces of paper. Go ahead and wad up each piece of paper and "pack" it into a suitcase or backpack. Give yourself time to carry it around or leave it by your back door, as though you were going on a trip. After prayer and some time that you decide, open the suitcase or backpack, unwad each piece of paper and throw it in the garbage. Return your luggage back into storage, remembering that you no longer have to carry that "garbage" around with you. Ahhh!

"For my yoke is easy and my burden is light." — Matthew 11:30

25. BURY YOUR BITTERNESS; GROW SOMETHING BEAUTIFUL

Find a spot around your home, garden, or neighboring woods, and dig a hole as deeply as signifies the depth of your pain caused by your negative emotions. Take some time to gaze into that hole as though it was your soul. Think about what you want to come from your heart and soul, understanding that out of negative thoughts come negative actions, and out of positive thoughts come positive actions. In the hole, plant some sort of beautiful plant or flower. Perhaps a succulent represents the person or situation that has "sucked the life out of you" in the past. Cover the roots with the surrounding dirt, water the plant or flower, and say a prayer of blessing that the plant or flower will plant roots into the dirt and grow to be a beautiful part of your environment, just as your heart and soul will plant roots into the holiness that comes from forgiveness and restoration to be a more beautiful part of your being. When that bitterness wants to grow back into your thoughts, remind yourself that you are nurturing something new and different into that space, and you no longer have the time or space for it any more.

> *Sow righteousness for yourselves, reap the fruit of unfailing love, and break up your unplowed ground; for it is time to seek the Lord, until he comes and showers his righteousness on you.*
> —Hosea 10:12

26. READ AND MEDITATE ON SCRIPTURES ABOUT BITTERNESS AND FORGIVENESS.
We can search the word "forgive" in the Bible and receive wisdom about letting go of hurt and disappointment, but Jesus' words to his disciples describe and expand his way for us to live in peace.

Matthew Chapter 6:1-34 (NIV)
> *"Be careful not to practice your righteousness in front of others to be seen by them. If you do, you will have no reward from your Father in heaven. "So when you give to the needy, do not announce it with trumpets, as the hypocrites do in the synagogues and on the streets, to be honored by others. Truly I tell you, they have received their reward in full. But when you give to the needy, do not let your left hand know what your right hand is doing, so that your giving may be in secret. Then your Father, who sees what is done in secret, will reward you.*

PRAYER
> *"And when you pray, do not be like the hypocrites, for they love to pray standing in the synagogues and on the street corners to be seen by others. Truly I tell you, they have received their reward in full. But when you pray, go into your room, close the door and pray to your Father, who is unseen. Then your Father, who sees what is done in secret, will reward you. And when you pray, do not keep on babbling like pagans, for they think they will be heard because of their many words. Do not be like them, for your Father knows what you need before you ask him.*

> *"This, then, is how you should pray:*

> *"'Our Father in heaven,*
> *hallowed be your name,*
> *your kingdom come,*
> *your will be done,*

> *on earth as it is in heaven.*
> *Give us today our daily bread.*
> *And forgive us our debts,*
> *as we also have forgiven our debtors.*
> *And lead us not into temptation,*
> *but deliver us from the evil one.*

For if you forgive other people when they sin against you, your heavenly Father will also forgive you. But if you do not forgive others their sins, your Father will not forgive your sins.

FASTING

"When you fast, do not look somber as the hypocrites do, for they disfigure their faces to show others they are fasting. Truly I tell you, they have received their reward in full. But when you fast, put oil on your head and wash your face, so that it will not be obvious to others that you are fasting, but only to your Father, who is unseen; and your Father, who sees what is done in secret, will reward you.

Treasures in Heaven
"Do not store up for yourselves treasures on earth, where moths and vermin destroy, and where thieves break in and steal. But store up for yourselves treasures in heaven, where moths and vermin do not destroy, and where thieves do not break in and steal. For where your treasure is, there your heart will be also.

"The eye is the lamp of the body. If your eyes are healthy, your whole body will be full of light. But if your eyes are unhealthy, your whole body will be full of darkness. If then the light within you is darkness, how great is that darkness!

"No one can serve two masters. Either you will hate the one and love the other, or you will be devoted to the one and despise the other. You cannot serve both God and money.

DO NOT WORRY

"Therefore I tell you, do not worry about your life, what you will eat or drink; or about your body, what you will wear. Is not life more than food, and the body more than clothes? Look at the birds of the air; they do not sow or reap or store away in barns, and yet your

heavenly Father feeds them. Are you not much more valuable than they? Can any one of you by worrying add a single hour to your life. "And why do you worry about clothes? See how the flowers of the field grow. They do not labor or spin. Yet I tell you that not even Solomon in all his splendor was dressed like one of these. If that is how God clothes the grass of the field, which is here today and tomorrow is thrown into the fire, will he not much more clothe you— you of little faith? So do not worry, saying, 'What shall we eat?' or 'What shall we drink?' or 'What shall we wear?' For the pagans run after all these things, and your heavenly Father knows that you need them. But seek first his kingdom and his righteousness, and all these things will be given to you as well. Therefore do not worry about tomorrow, for tomorrow will worry about itself. Each day has enough trouble of its own."

27. FLIP YOUR SCRIPT! THE POWER OF YOUR WORDS

Words have the power to motivate or deflate others and ourselves. If we always run a negative script in our minds about anger, betrayal, disappointment, and all the other negative emotions, we will continue to be negative and maybe even feel worse. However, if we run a positive script in our minds every day that infuses hope, joy, love, faithfulness, and forgiveness, we will become positive people who feel better about ourselves and others.

Instead of saying to yourself (or aloud), "I hope (_____) rots in hell for what they did to me," try saying and feeling, "I don't understand what could have caused (_____) to do that to me, but I hope that one day we can come to a resolve and live together in heaven for eternity." Seriously, what is God going to do with all the people who say they love Jesus but can't get along with each other? When it's time to go to heaven, does God have enough mansions and streets of gold to separate all the Christians who love Jesus but don't love their fellow brothers and sisters? Maybe we can't get a mansion until we make friends with our enemies. Whoa! Is that worth heaven? I think so!

28. "YOU'RE NO JESUS CHRIST"

No matter how much people or situations have hurt you and caused you to feel bitterness, compare your life to the life that Jesus Christ lived and died. Did you suffer more than Jesus, who was wrongly accused, was tortured, suffered immense pain from nails in his hands and feet and a crown of thorns pressed into the flesh of his head and face? Were you entirely innocent of all sin, yet spat on and shamed publicly with lies and injustice? No matter what you have suffered, or no matter what loss you have experienced, when you compare it to that of Jesus Christ, your situation pales by comparison. Yes, you were hurt. Yes, you were or are suffering, but you are no Jesus Christ. Yet he forgave all wrongdoing even as he was suffering and close to death by saying,

"Father, forgive them, for they know not what they are doing."
— Luke 23:24

Perhaps you are thinking, "Yes, but I suffer at the hands of those who know what they are doing." Whether you have been hurt intentionally or unintentionally, wrongdoers do not really know the extent of how much pain they are inflicting, nor what causes them to want to hurt someone else.

When I think of the corporal punishment that I inflicted on my children, which was spanking, I have deep regret, because I have since learned more effective ways to correct children's behavior without physically hurting them. When I think of the corporal punishment that my father inflicted on my siblings and me, I wince, still feeling the sting of the physical hurt and the emotional hurt coming from someone who was supposed to love me unconditionally. However, when I think of the level of physical abuse and emotional abuse that my father suffered at the hands of his parents, I find myself feeling sympathy and pity for him. I realized that he had actually improved in his disciplinary methods from those used by his parents.

Imagine being a young child tied to a tree in the front of your house because you wet the bed, and as long as the sheets were being laundered and hung on the clothes line, you were confined and subject to public ridicule. As your friends pass by and ask why you are tied to the tree, you remain silent, but your mother shouts from the house, "Go ahead! Tell them that you wet the bed!" How awful for my father, not only to experience this as a child, but to learn such horrible parenting skills like this. Tragically, smacks across the face for the girls and belt whippings for the boys in my family were improvements in the family cycle. When I became a parent, I regretfully resorted to spankings and just one smack on the face of a smart-mouthed teen, but then learned kinder ways to redirect behaviors. Fortunately, the next generation of parents learned that simply using consequences, such as reducing the number of books read at bedtime, resulted in corrected behaviors from their children.

When I feel any bitterness toward my father, I remember that the days of my youth were different times and a different culture of parenting, and more importantly, none of these punishments came one iota close to the pain and suffering by Jesus Christ, not by any sin committed by him, but for all of the sins of the world placed on his shoulders. He swallowed the most bitter pill and was able to forgive without malice toward his enemies. Thank God that I have not suffered to that extreme. Thank God that I am no Jesus Christ, merely a follower of him, my Savior.

And the God of all grace, who called you to his eternal glory in Christ, after you have suffered a little while, will himself restore you and make you strong, firm and steadfast. —1 Peter 5:10

29. IDENTIFY AND THWART OFF ANY "BITTER TRIGGERS"

Any words or actions that are part of a past bitter experience may resurface in unexpected ways that may cause a healed wound to reopen if we are not careful to identify just what those things may be. For example, when our sons were young, we would have regular "family meetings" for everyone to talk about life together, the good and the not-so-good happenings. However, after a major event when our boys had disappeared from our sight for what seemed to be an eternity in order to chase an ice cream truck roving our neighborhood, a family meeting was called. I am not so sure that I had facilitated that meeting with calm and patience, and the resulting consequence was that we would never purchase ice cream from the Mister Softee truck again...ever! With such an extreme, albeit unreasonable, response, our boys dreaded any talk of a family meeting after that. Just the phrase "family meeting" still causes a shudder from our adult sons who are parents themselves now. For me, just the "ding" of a traveling ice cream truck pokes at my emotions.

Other examples of a "bitter trigger" might be the following:

(Check to see if yours is listed.)

"Can we talk?"

"Hey, can I ask you something?"

"That's something your mother/father would have done."

"The family Christmas party is coming up."

"I remember when you used to...."

A funeral

A wedding

A scene in a movie

Teasing or bullying

A siren or loud noise

Trauma anniversary dates (that your body remembers when your mind forgets)

The principal's office or the boss's office

Did I hit on any of yours? For some people, events like weddings or Christmas may exude positive feelings. Even a funeral can evoke a positive emotion if the event was a wonderful tribute with warm expressions of sympathy. Wisdom is identifying what triggers may try to take you back to former feelings of bitterness and being prepared to tap into your logical brain power. Remind yourself of your present state of resolve without a desire to relive any past bitterness or disappointment. Then sing your version of "Let It Go" and move your thoughts forward.

It is better to be patient than to fight. It is better to control your temper than to take a city. — Proverbs 16:32

Lamentations 3 is a good reminder that vengeance belongs to the Lord as he so chooses. As Jeremiah cried out to the Lord, he also asked God to pay his enemies back for what their hands have done and to pursue them in anger and destroy them.

Payback is God's prerogative, not ours. Once we have forgiven our transgressors, we need to pray for them, try to understand them, or take steps to forget about them rather than dwelling on the hurts and afflictions from them. Constantly remembering how we were hurt only replicates the pain and disappointment on some level.

One dark recess of my soul that I recently discovered was a reaction that surfaced when I learned that one of my transgressors had suffered a setback in life. I felt a little joyful that "payback" had "finally" happened while I was still around to witness it. I remember thinking something like, "It's about time they got what they had coming to them," or "I wonder how that feels, now that the shoe is on the other foot?" or "Oh, karma" (even though I don't believe in karma as a religious belief). Any number of snarky responses ran through my brain. I was not living the embodiment of Philippians 4:8.

Finally, brothers and sisters, whatever is true, whatever is noble, whatever is right, whatever is pure, whatever is lovely, whatever is admirable—if anything is excellent or praiseworthy—think about such things. — Philippians 4:8

As I have been reflecting deeply about unknown recesses of bitterness in my heart, I realize that any joy at another person's suffering is not of God; it is not how Jesus would have responded; and it is not healthy for me. It is not pure, lovely, admirable, excellent, nor praiseworthy. Only God can judge, and only God can decide what a person deserves, good or bad.

If I am to be healed completely of all bitterness, then I must put my heart in check when I hear of a current or former transgressor's trials, setbacks, disappointments, or failures. Regardless of how I was hurt by them, I must leave room for God to work in their lives, perhaps transforming them and guiding them to a better place long after their former selves had treated me unfairly. People can change, and God can change people. I try to repeat that to myself when I hear of the misfortune of former transgressors. "People can change, and God can change people."

If God had paid me back what I deserve for all the times that I have mistreated others or have caused pain, grief, heartache, disappointment, or harm, surely I would be "destroyed from under the heavens of the Lord."

30. SEEK PROFESSIONAL AND/OR PASTORAL ASSISTANCE. DO THE RESEARCH. GIVE YOURSELF A SECOND CHANCE.

Research available counselors, psychologists, or life coaches to help when bitterness is all-consuming or debilitating. Breaking out of bitterness is life changing.

Set an appointment with your pastor or regular spiritual advisor for initial and ongoing conversations to help with accountability and further advice.

A heart that understands what is right looks for knowledge. But the mouths of foolish people feed on what is foolish."
— Proverbs 15:14 (NIRV)

CHAPTER SIX

"Overcoming Bitterness"

by Three Modern Women

What Present Day Writers Say About Overcoming Bitterness

RACHEL BANE'S STORY

One of the problems with bitterness is it can be sneaky. Bitterness can hide in various ways, and we may not even realize it. One day while praying, I asked, "Why do I feel this way, Lord? Why is this happening to me?" I was shocked at God's response. One word: bitterness. My tears that followed that revelation were bitter as well. There's a reason the Apostle Paul says in 2 Corinthians 7:10, "Godly sorrow brings repentance that leads to salvation and leaves no regret, but worldly sorrow brings death."

I grabbed my journal to write down the thoughts that were racing in my mind. I was astounded at all of the things I wrote down that had hurt me, or were still currently troubling me. I had allowed these hurts to take root in my heart, and out of the root of hurt, grew bitterness. Wow, I was bitter. How did I not recognize this in my life? My heart ached. Bitterness had manifested itself outwardly and showed up as unforgiveness, depressed moments, and a cynical spirit. The root of bitterness had been keeping me stuck from moving forward.

Once God revealed to me that the underlying problem was bitterness, I began to repent. I asked God to forgive me for allowing bitterness into my heart and mind. I asked God to rip out the root ball of bitterness and replace the bitterness with praise and thanksgiving. I've always been the girl that practiced gratitude. Maybe that's why it was so shocking to me. I couldn't believe I had "secretly" been bitter all along. Do I still get hurt today? Absolutely and unfortunately. I wish I could tell you that hurt will never come, but the reality is we are all flawed humans. God will equip us to overcome painful moments and circumstances.

Will we have the courage to quiet our busy lives and ask God, "God, are there any areas in my heart that bitterness has taken root?" Will we be still and listen for the Holy Spirit to reveal an answer to us? We have a choice. Will we choose to remain hurt and hindered, or will we move forward in the freedom and healing that Christ has for us? God has a better plan for us than bitterness.

The choice is up to us how we proceed. I pray that you choose the path of praise over pain and bitterness. God created you for much more than living from a place of woundedness. I believe in you and the power of God to remove bitterness from your life. You are worthy of healing and goodness.

GEA JONES-THOMPSON'S TESTIMONY

Ever have a wound that is healing, and then something rubs against it? The same feeling of irritation, pain, and discomfort that you feel is what happens to me when I am reminded of the different events in my life that have left scars. Each event has affected me mentally, emotionally, physically, as well as spiritually. Many questions flood my mind, like what have I done to experience this? What could I have done differently to achieve another outcome? As I think of the things that have caused me to experience feelings of bitterness throughout my life, I can honestly say that I am still working on accepting the fact that everything happens for a reason.

Bitterness has presented itself on the regular when I envision something so much more. I know it is not advised to compare your life to others, but I know how I wanted my life to turn out. When it does not turn out the way I desired or imagined, it is hurtful. Is this right? NO. But this is honestly the way I feel. Even when God has shown me what it should be, and the enemy enters in to deter what is going on, I see how God uses bitterness to help me to grow to a higher level. After I had a chance to process the situation, it became apparent that it was time to change gears and start meditating on scriptures to combat the feelings that have caused me to become angry, bitter, and resentful. One such scripture is Romans 14:4 (GNT)…"And they will succeed, because the Lord is able to make them succeed." I love this scripture and choose to meditate on it because it's a gentle reminder that God has created me to succeed. No matter what I face, the trials I've overcome or the plans that didn't happen as expected, I know God has built me to succeed.

One of my hobbies is watching documentaries. It encourages me to see how an individual has gone through some of life's difficulties and learn how they have overcome them. Recently, I watched an autobiography on Quincy Jones, and at one point he shared, "Not one drop of my self-worth depends on your acceptance of me." This quote was such a fresh reminder that I am enough! It reminded me that my self-worth is not predicated on anyone else's opinion of me but God's. I hope this quote can be the same reminder to you.

Here are four ways to better overcome bitterness. First, you must acknowledge what it is that is causing you to feel bitterness. In addition to bitterness, we can experience feelings of anger, disappointment, and resentment. Second, you must meditate on God's word. This is important because it helps us to take our eyes off the problem and focus on God, who is the solution. It's also important because through God's word we are focusing on his voice and not our own or the enemy's. Through the Bible, God shows us how beautiful and precious we are to HIM; seeing this allows us to also decrease the negative self-talk we might experience. Third, you must find an outlet. An outlet can be a hobby you enjoy doing. This is important because it helps to release and heal your emotions. Fourth, you must realize that God is in the situation and knows what you need even if you don't see or understand it at the time. Remember that God created you in your mother's womb.

> *For you formed my innermost parts; you knit me together in my mother's womb. I will give thanks and praise to You for I am fearfully and wonderfully made; Wonderfully are Your works, and my soul knows it very well.* — Psalms 139:13-16 (AMP)

TESTIMONY FROM LIFE COACH ERICA WILLIAMS

Before I was born, my mom and dad had a difficult time with my sister (juvenile delinquent starting at birth) and did not want another child. Surprise! My Mom got pregnant with me. She had a difficult pregnancy. Because she was in pain the entire pregnancy, on pain medication, and stressed from many things, my brain reserve was already being depleted.

What is brain reserve? Even before you were conceived, your parents' habits were laying the foundation for your overall physical, mental, and brain health. At conception, your brain had amazing potential for brain reserve. Some of us have more reserve than

others, and we can tolerate or we can withstand insults to our brain. Brain reserve is the extra brain tissue or function you have available to deal with whatever stress comes your way. If a mother is healthy, doesn't have chronic stress, isn't exposed to chemicals, then she is building our brain reserve; and the opposite is true. Our birth experience, upbringing, home environment, food, physical injuries, etc. continue to either add to our brain reserve or decrease it. As adults, we continue to add or decrease our brain reserve.

Early in my mother's pregnancy, she prayed that God would show her or give her a sign that I was going to be ok, going to be healthy. God showed her that during an ultrasound when the doctor said that my head was the most perfectly shaped head he had ever seen. Mom said she knew that the Lord had something special planned for me, for my life, but we all know that when that happens, life is not going to be easy.

And it hasn't been. The list of traumas and disappointments I've had in life..a normal/healthy person would say "I wouldn't wish that on my worst enemy.." the bitter me would say "I would wish that on my worst enemy." I have spent decades being angry, hurt, and disappointed at God. My personality is black/white, practical/analytical—I don't do well with theories. I need facts, I need visuals, I need tactile. Well, God doesn't work like that.

I was saved at the age of 4 at the dinner table praying for the food and baptized at the age of 5. Over the years many people have said that is too young and I didn't really know what I was believing, OR they say, "Well, then, you really haven't led the life of someone who appreciates salvation." In many ways the latter of the two is true, but in many ways, it's been harder because I have lived a life different from the majority of my peers and didn't see the blessing from it.

I also lived more of my life knowing the right and wrong and the consequences, so when I did wrong, my guilt was deeper and impactful; and when I saw others doing wrong, I went into judgment mode, again a sin about which I felt guilty.

BITTER TO BETTER

I used to have the memory of an elephant and can tell you every wrong ever done to me and every wrong I've ever done. What a burden this has been.

90's Tribulation Videos
1. Not trusting
2. Always watching
3. True definition of conspiracy theorist
4. Worried about future
5. Prayed and worried that God would come back before I was married
6. I guess I "knew" early on that would come true
7. In college my roommates were the epitome of horrible roommates. At the time I hated it and fell into depression, BUT it also led me to get closer to God. In my Bible you will find R'96 next to so many verses that the Holy Spirit spoke through to me. It caused me to crave God, to lean in so I could hear Him speak, but also He was someone I could cry out to and ask for discernment for understanding and comfort.
8. In my 20's, I was diagnosed with PCOS (PolyCystic Ovary Syndrome) and was told I would never have kids. I won't go into all the horrible things that come along with PCOS, but let me tell you, to this day I have to daily ask the Lord to take away the hurt and bitterness that overwhelms me.
9. All I ever wanted was to be married and have a child
10. God had another plan
11. Spiritual warfare
12. As a child, I had a nightmare where I "woke up" to angels and demons fighting over my bed.
13. My life verses have been James 1:2-4 (NIV): *Consider it pure joy, my brothers and sisters, whenever you face trials of many kinds, 3 because you know that the testing of your faith produces perseverance. 4 Let perseverance finish its work so that you may be mature and complete, not lacking anything.*
14. I joke about comparing my life to Job's life. Then I feel guilty: how could I dare compare my life to Job's? And when I started working with combat veterans that were missing 1-4 limbs, eyesight, etc., I felt even guiltier being bitter at God. My troubles were NOTHING compared to theirs.

For years I have begged God to take the anxiety and depression away. I just wanted to be normal. It wasn't until 2013 that I took a course from Dr. Daniel Amen when he used the phrase, "What if Mental Health is really Brain Health?" That intrigued me. He also talks about being healthy or sick in 4 circles: Biological, Psychological, Social, and Spiritual. When any of those is unhealthy or lacking, the other 3 suffer.

I had been on anxiety depression medication for 23 years with no healing in sight. In fact, my emotions were like a roller coaster: a lot of downs, numb/robot-like days, others where I couldn't cry if I wanted to, even when "needing to" over the death of family/friend; lots of side effects. I prayed and cried to God that I just wanted to be normal, I wanted to be healed. I've had decades of "WHY????" prayers and screams to God. Why me, why not me, why now, why not now, etc.?

After taking the course, I followed Dr. Amen's suggestions and was able to be off all prescribed medications. With the biological circle, he explained that if your biology is unhealthy, that can cause or mimic psychological disorders that are everyday diagnosed and given medicine without ever looking at the underlying cause. Case in point: I have had several traumatic brain injuries; my hormones are out of whack; my thyroid is not healthy; and my cortisol levels are off the charts. All of these separate or combined would mimic Severe anxiety, Major depressive disorder, ADD, and several other "mental disorders." This would have confirmed my idea that something was wrong with my mind, that I was weak in my spiritual life, etc. However, in reality, I needed to heal my brain. (See Appendix for Amen Clinics Suggested Blood Panel.)

The psychological circle has to do with upbringing, traumatic events, i.e. how I think about myself. With anxiety and depression and PTSD, all of my thoughts are negative, distrusting, feeling everything I do is wrong. Again, that must mean I am not serving God right, or I am not trusting Him. The social circle is how strong is our connection to people, how stressful is our job, how stressed are we with finances, etc. Again, all of those are impacted when our brain is not healthy.

The spiritual circle has to do with our connection to God (or something higher). What is our meaning, our purpose? Why am I here? All of that was impacted because my brain wasn't healthy.

BITTER TO BETTER

At the beginning of this year, I was in a ladies Bible study. We were working through Fully Alive by Susie Larson, and in the first or second week, we read Psalm 23 (NIV).

The Lord is my shepherd, I lack nothing.

He makes me lie down in green pastures,
he leads me beside quiet waters,

He refreshes my soul.
He guides me along the right paths
*   for his name's sake.*

Even though I walk
*   through the darkest valley,*
I will fear no evil,
*   for you are with me;*
your rod and your staff,
*   they comfort me.*

You prepare a table before me
*   in the presence of my enemies.*
You anoint my head with oil;
*   my cup overflows.*

Surely your goodness and love will follow me
*   all the days of my life,*
and I will dwell in the house of the Lord forever.

DAILY I have to CHOOSE not to be bitter. DAILY I have to CHOOSE to trust that God is working everything in my life for HIS purpose. My mom is forever reminding me, DAILY I have to say, "What pleases you, pleases me." Or "DISappointment = HISappointment" (As Silver Refined by Kay Arthur). DAILY I have to ask forgiveness for any bitterness that creeps into my thoughts. Being Bitter hasn't gotten me anywhere...but I want to be a Better Christian, a Better Single Woman, a Better Daughter, Aunt, Sister, and a Better Friend. If I am BITTER I am of no use to God or my clients. If I hadn't gone through everything in my past and present, then how effective would I be for my clients?

Lately, two different authors have said we need to read the Bible to learn about God and to know what He was doing and why versus reading it trying to see how it relates to my life. That struck me like nothing before. I lived my life waiting for the next shoe to drop or waiting for the rug to be pulled out from under me. Sometimes trauma looks like not being able to count your blessings or get your hopes up or be excited about something because you are too afraid that it is going to be taken from you or the rug is going to be pulled out from under you. To the outside world, sometimes it looks like you are ungrateful or you are depressed or you are upset, when in reality, you are just trying to protect your heart from more disappointment.

I read this from Caroline Middlesdorf on Instagram: "POV the desire for a stress fresh start, running away, or making drastic life changes is actually a trauma response. Making drastic changes can be your way of coping, attempting to escape or to distance yourself from the emotional triggers and reminders linked to your past trauma. Trauma often involves a loss of control period. The impulse to make drastic life changes is your attempt to regain a sense of control over your life, providing a semblance of order in the chaos and stress you may have experienced. The desire for a fresh start is often closely tied to your deep need for safety. Trauma can erode your sense of safety, and the pursuit of new beginnings is your effort to create a space that feels secure, free from the threat and vulnerabilities associated with your past traumatic experiences. Trauma can really shatter your sense of self. Making significant life changes is your attempt to reconstruct and redefine your identity apart from the negative impact of your past experiences. Facing unresolved trauma can be emotionally overwhelming. The impulse to run away or make drastic changes is your way to avoid confronting and processing the painful emotions linked to your past. Trauma often shapes a negative life narrative. Making major life changes is your active effort to transform this narrative. You are looking to create a more positive and empowering story for lying for yourself. The unknown can be for some less intimidating than the known trauma. Seeking novelty through new experiences provides you with a distraction, diverting your attention from the distressing past memories and emotions. While a fresh start and changes can be beneficial, if it becomes a repetitive cycle and pattern in your life, it means that you are actually running away from yourself. Instead of healing, you keep on trying to avoid introspection and processing the surfacing emotions linked to your past trauma. Can you relate?"

The reason why this stood out so much for me is that I am forever moving. I moved every year to a different dorm or apartment in college. I have moved to different cities, I have changed jobs so many times; I have changed churches, etc. etc., always thinking the next move will be the one where I am happy. The next move is where I will find my Prince Charming. The next move will be the one when I find my best friend. The next move will be finding "the career", the one that will give me money to retire on and travel the world. Then one day, I heard a quote from The Graveyard Book by Neil Gaiman: "It's like the people who believe they'll be happy if they go and live somewhere else, but who learn it doesn't work that way. Wherever you go, you take yourself with you."

That resonated so much with me because it's right. If I'm not healing, then I'm still taking the broken part of me with me every time I move. I'm still taking the same person. Just because the environment or the city has changed, I have not. Why do I think I will change with the move?

In January I was hospitalized for shortness of breath. After going through an extensive series of tests, I was discharged from the hospital. After 41/2 days in the hospital, the doctors could not find "anything wrong," so they had to discharge me. One of the tests showed a large mass on my ovary, but no one seemed concerned. After several months of tests, the doctors determined that there was a high probability of cancer.

After reading the tests results and meeting with the oncologist, believe it or not, I was fine. I thought, if it is cancer and "terminal", then I am so ready to go to Heaven. If it's not terminal, then God will definitely be using this for His Glory. Either way, I was at peace. Now there were days when a sudden burst of anxiety or crying would overwhelm me, but I had to remind myself that nothing happens in our life without it going through God's hands first. Not once did I get mad at God! I know that God had me go to the ER for breathing, because I would not have found the mass or the cancer without that trip to the ER.

During my surgery more tests were done, and no cancer was found! I don't know why I had to go through this, but I know God gave me another chance to see Him work and to look forward to seeing how He will use this in my life.

(See Appendix for Relaxation Techniques, Amen Clinics Suggested Blood Panel, and Adult ANT Therapy)

Research from Dr. Daniel Amen, submitted by Erica Williams:

Erica Williams
Owner, Life Coach
8050 Beckett Center Dr. Suite 211
West Chester, OH 45069
513.874.LIFE(5433) | www.lifecca.com

From Dr. Amen's books, clinics, courses, or the website:

"If you have crushing chest pain, your doctor will scan your heart; but if you have crushing depression, no one will ever look at your brain.

If you are sick to your stomach, your doctor will image your abdomen; but if you are sick with anxiety, no one will ever look at your brain.

If you have stabbing back pain, your doctor will order an MRI; but if you have urges to stab others, no one will ever look at your brain.

If you have persistent knee pain, your doctor will image your knees; but if you have persistent heartache, no one will ever look at your brain.

If you have a chronic cough, your doctor will X-ray your chest; but if alcoholic behavior is ruining your life, no one will ever look at your brain.

If you have tormenting hip pain, your doctor will scan your hip; but if you torment your spouse so much that he or she leaves you, no one will ever look at your brain.

If you were paralyzed from an accident, your doctor will scan your spine; but if you are paralyzed with obsessive thoughts, no one will ever look at your brain.

If you develop a runaway tachycardia, your doctor will scan your heart; but if your teenager runs away and lives on the street, no one will ever look at his or her brain.

Psychiatry remains the only medical specialty that virtually never looks at the organ it treats.

You have heard it said that a picture is worth 1000 words but a map is worth 1000 images. Without a map you are lost. If you're lost in the wilderness without a map, you unnecessarily suffer and are at risk of dying. Likewise, many people are lost in the morass of psychiatric care, and the lack of proper diagnosis and treatment cost many people their lives . In (2023) this is simply unacceptable."

Dr. Daniel Amen "The End of Mental Illness"

"Stuck at a traffic light midday at the corner of Hollywood and Vine in Hollywood CA on my way to record a podcast, I saw a 30 something man with dirty blonde hair, ripped clothes, and blood on his face, talking to himself while gesturing wildly in the air.

He seemed oblivious to everyone around him, and those walking on the street paid him no mind. After all, this was Hollywood and Vine. Most of my colleagues would have diagnosed him with schizophrenia or unstable bipolar disorder and wondered why he wasn't taking his medication to help the voices and visions stay away.

When I saw him, I wondered when he'd had his last brain injury, if he had been exposed to mold or environmental toxins, if he suffered with severe gut health issues, or whether he had an infectious disease like Lyme or toxoplasmosis ravaging his brain."

Dr. Daniel Amen "The End of Mental Illness"

"Walking into my California clinic one day and my office manager quickly pulled me aside and said, 'Daniel you have to see Tommy.' I let her know that I already had fourteen people on my schedule, but she just dismissed me and said, 'Daniel, you need to see Tommy. He's really cute; he's nine years old; and he's read your book, *Change Your Brain Change Your Life.*'

OK a nine year old who read my book, now I was paying attention. I found Tommy in one of the other doctor's offices. The young boy saw me. He yelled, 'Hey, you're Dr. Amen!' What he said next absolutely floored me.

'Dr. Amen, I have a left temporal lobe problem.'

'Really,' I asked, 'How do you know?'

He said he had taken the checklist in the book. 'I have a really bad temper and you write that people who have bad tempers often have temporal lobe problems.'

He was right. Then he added, 'And I used to see ghosts.'

I asked him what he meant. He said, 'I used to see these green things floating in front of my eyes. I thought they were ghosts, and they would scare me until I read your book and realized they were just illusions that people with temporal lobe problems get.'

Then he looked at me with his big beautiful blue eyes and said, "Last year, to get rid of the bad thoughts in my head, I tried to kill myself.'

The thought of this sweet young boy trying to kill himself because he thought he was seeing monsters broke my heart, but he was right. People who have temporal lobe problems do tend to have dark, evil, awful thoughts. I think of them as mindstorms, and sadly, people who suffer from them often try to kill themselves."

Dr. Daniel Amen "The End of Mental Illness"

Resources by Dr. Daniel Amen: *"Conquering Anxiety & Depression"*, *"Change Your Brain, Change Your Life"*, *"Your Brain is Always Listening,"* 6-week group called *"Overcoming, Anxiety, Depression, Trauma, & Grief"* with Dr. Amen

CHAPTER SEVEN

One Man's Miracle

MATT NICOL'S TESTIMONY

Matt Nicol teaches social studies in Hamilton City Schools, Ohio. Beyond school, he works with youth in Christian settings and often gives his testimony at gatherings. If you have ever felt bitter about life's circumstances, Matt's testimony will encourage you to change your perspective by relying on God. I first saw a Facebook post on October 21, 2011:

For those that don't know, last night I was diagnosed with a tumor on the left side of my brain. They are admitting me to University Hospital in Cincinnati this evening and will begin running tests and looking at the courses of action. We will find out answers to questions and it is a blessing that they were able to take me right away.

More than anything, whether you are family, church family, friends, former students, or colleagues, I love you all deeply and entrust myself fully to the healing power of God through Jesus Christ, through whom all things are possible!! My faith and life is always in His hands and none other. I believe strongly in the power of prayer and that God can heal me to be a witness. I'm all in with that trust and my prayer and hope is that all of you place your faith and trust in Him!

We will set up a care page with updates and will update people in that way. Our biggest request now is prayer, prayer, and more prayer!! Pray that the tumor is benign, can be treated, and for healing. Pray for my family and for me to be a source of strength for them, as I know it is hard to go through. Pray for my students. I told my AP Euro class today and I asked for their prayers and many took it hard.

Thank you to all!

Matt

The LORD your God is with you,
 the Mighty Warrior who saves.
He will take great delight in you;
 in his love he will no longer rebuke you,
 but will rejoice over you with singing.—Zephaniah 3:17

During the writing of this book, I saw more posts from Matt, now 12 years later.

Facebook Post: October 8, 2023

Where you are each day is your battleground! Make sure you go into the trenches with your armor of protection! The Word needs to be in your heart! Speak life into those around you! Be bold, believer! Don't let the enemy get into your head because He cannot prevail!

For we do not wrestle against flesh and blood, but against principalities, against powers, against the rulers of the darkness of this age, against spiritual hosts of wickedness in the heavenly places. Therefore take up the whole armor of God, that you may be able to withstand in the evil day, and having done all, to stand.
—Ephesians 6:12-13 (NKJV)

Facebook Post: October 15, 2023

Then He said to His disciples, "The harvest truly is plentiful, but the laborers are few. Therefore pray the Lord of the harvest to send out laborers into His harvest." —Matthew 9:37-38 (NKJV)

God is a God of multiplication, not division!

Are you the cause of division or are you in a position to be used to multiply the Kingdom where you are? Are you allowing the Holy Spirit to speak to you, through you, and overflow from you? Are you seeing those around you as Jesus sees them?

All I know is that I've seen angels surrounding the unlovable and Jesus holding them as they are down. I've seen the miracle of someone deemed not worth the effort come to be a powerful force for the kingdom. NO ONE is too far gone that they are unredeemable. A harvest is coming!! Are you ready?

For the Scripture says, 'Whoever believes on Him will not be put to shame.' For there is no distinction between Jew and Greek, for the same Lord over all is rich to all who call upon Him. For 'whoever calls on the name of the Lord shall be saved.' —Romans 10:11-13 (NKJV)

Facebook Post: October 21, 2023

12 years ago today was the day that rocked my world. I found out that I had a brain tumor. Five days later, I had surgery to remove it. The surgery was more complicated than they thought, and I woke up paralyzed on my right side. I had to learn to walk, talk, and do things that everybody has to do every day. There was still a piece of tumor embedded in my brain that they had to leave in there. Doctors wanted to watch it, instead of doing radiation to remove it.

Gradually, after doing extensive rehab, I was able to go back to work. About 4 1/2 months after the surgery, I felt symptoms and went in for an MRI. The tumor had disappeared! The only explanation was that God had completely healed me. Aside from scar tissue, the tumor has not returned, and I still feel the effects when the weather changes. We all have scars as reminders of what God has done for us, and mine just happens to be on my head!

God is still alive and working miracles! I see them every day! You never know, through a conversation or a kind gesture, when you will be the answer to someone else's prayer. I praise God for the good times, and the bad times, as challenges are now seen as opportunities to grow. So, I encourage everyone to praise God in the good and bad times, and to take chances and opportunities when they are presented to share what God has done for you! In all circumstances, He is there guiding you and walking through it with you!

Where can I go from Your Spirit? Or where can I flee from Your presence? If I ascend into heaven, You are there; If I make my bed in hell, behold, You are there. If I take the wings of the morning, And dwell in the uttermost parts of the sea, Even there Your hand shall lead me, And Your right hand shall hold me. —Psalms 139:7-10 (NKJV)

Email from October 24, 2023 when asking Matt how he battled any bitterness or disappointment in his life.

That is perfectly fine to copy my FB post!! When they removed the tumor, they went in and it affected my emotional center. One minute, I'd be happy and talking about Jesus. The next minute, I'd be angry and kick someone out of the room. Another, I'd be sad for missing my family. At times, I'd let my mind wander. (My pastor calls this the thoughts, ideals, and suggestions that the enemy uses against us.) I would say I was grateful to be alive and at peace.

Philippians 4:6-7 "Be anxious for nothing, but in everything by prayer and supplication, with thanksgiving, let your requests be made known to God; and the peace of God, which surpasses all *understanding, will guard your hearts and minds through Christ Jesus."*

When I was in the pre-op area, waiting to be rolled into surgery. They were delayed and I was freaking out. My wife and pastor came in and my pastor at the time started praying over me and there was immediate peace, to the point where I was cracking jokes with the surgeon as they were wheeling me into the operating room. The peace that only the Holy Spirit can give filled the room. I don't think I fully realized how much rehab I would have to do, even when paralyzed, due to God's peace. I had to relearn how to walk, talk, and do basic things.....feed myself....shower myself.......Anyway, that is that.

Matt's Written Testimony - More Details of This Miracle!

For I know the plans I have for you," declares the Lord, "plans to prosper you and not to harm you, plans to give you hope and a future. Then you will call on me and come and pray to me, and I will listen to you. You will seek me and find me when you seek me with all your heart. —Jeremiah 29:11-13

God's Peace and Redemption

My story begins about a year before my diagnosis: October / November 2010. Every now and then, I would get headaches and feel tingly numbness in one side of my head. I'd wake up in the middle of the night and my arm would be numb. I went to have it checked out and my doctor ordered all of these tests and everything came back normal. The only test not ordered was an MRI. I attributed it to laying on my arm. This went on for about almost a year.

In early October 2011, I was at a Starfield concert and we were sitting about 6 rows from the speaker and I had to go into the lobby because my head hurt really bad. That was not normal because I normally had gone to concerts in the past and the loudness never caused that to happen. All of that time I had been playing guitar in the praise band at church and I felt like I had drifted from God's presence, not feeling the Holy Spirit. I was going through the motions. Then, soon after, my friend and colleague, Duane Moore, almost died with 98% blockage in his heart and it made me ponder. I prayed to God shortly after: "God, I need to feel close to you again. Please, reveal yourself to me in a new way to let me know you are there." A few days later, a man of God from our church, Tim Brown, had a massive stroke and died, making me ponder again. I had a student teacher at that time and what follows is the sequence of events that changed everything.

The day after Tim Brown died, in the middle of my 2nd bell class, I suddenly went blind. The room was spinning and I struggled next door to Duane's room. He had just come back from his health issue. He and a student helped me to the nurse's office, and I regained my sight. My blood pressure was taken and it was pretty high. Later that day, I had an appointment with my doctor and more blood work was taken, and he also ordered an MRI. I went to get the MRI done on Thursday, October 20, 2011. Once it was over, they told me to wait and that my doctor wanted to see me later in the afternoon. My wife, Leah, met me at the doctor's office and my doctor, Dr. Niehaus, told us that I had what appeared to be a tumor in the center of my brain. He then said that he was sending it to the Mayfield Clinic associated with the University of Cincinnati and that they would contact me when it was time to go. We were speechless. I had a 6 and 4 year old at home. Were they going to be without a father? Was my wife, Leah, going to be without a husband? That night was a sleepless night.

The next day, I went to school like normal. I had a meeting with my principal, Dennis Malone, and told him what was going on and he stood up and gave me a hug and said a quick prayer. The only class that I kept during the time of having a student teacher was my AP European History class. During their class, they were researching in the library, when I got a message that there was a phone call for me in the office. I took the call and it was my doctor, telling me that I needed to get down to UC as soon as possible because they had a room for me and they wanted to run further tests. I hung up the phone and went back to my class and called them together. I told them what was going on and by the time I was done, we were all crying. One of the things that I will never forget is that two of them laid hands on me and prayed for healing, strength and comfort.

When I got to UC, the surgeon, Dr. Mario Zuccarello came and showed me the MRI and exactly what they were going to do. I stayed the night and the next day, they gave me a full body MRI and found that the tumor had not spread to the rest of my body, so all indicators were that the tumor was benign. I went home and the next day was

Sunday, so I went to church, as normal. They called me up and the whole church came up to the front, laid hands on me, and prayed over me. I was ready to go.

On the day of the surgery, October 25, we arrived at the hospital very early and they were preparing me for surgery. The surgery was supposed to begin around 11:00. I was in the pre-op room and began to get nervous, as 11:00 approached and there was no sign that surgery was going to begin. I began to freak out and since only 2 people at a time could come in to visit, Leah and my pastor at the time, Dan McDowell, came in and began to pray over me. What happened can be best described in the following verses from Philippians.

> *Rejoice in the Lord always. Again I will say, rejoice! Let your gentleness be known to all men. The Lord is at hand. Be anxious for nothing, but in everything by prayer and supplication, with thanksgiving, let your requests be made known to God; and the peace of God, which surpasses all understanding, will guard your hearts and minds through Christ Jesus.* — **Philippians 4: 4-7**

I don't remember what Pastor Dan prayed; all I remember was feeling total peace. I was submitted to God's will, whatever that may be.

> *I am crucified with Christ: nevertheless I live; yet not I, but Christ lives in me: and the life which I now live in the flesh I live by the faith of the Son of God, who loved me, and gave himself for me.* —Galatians 2:20 NKJV

The surgery did not begin until 2:30 or so, and to give an idea of how much at peace that I was, they wheeled me in and my surgeon asked, "How are you feeling, Matt?" I replied, "The question is 'how are you feeling because if you are not feeling well or you are tired, then maybe you shouldn't be working on my brain." The last thing I remember is that the whole operating room was laughing and Dr. Z said, "Put him under."

> *I will extol thee, O LORD; for thou hast lifted me up, and hast not made my foes to rejoice over me.*
>
> *O LORD my God, I cried unto thee, and thou hast healed me.*
>
> *O LORD, thou hast brought up my soul from the grave: thou hast kept me alive, that I should not go down to the pit.*

Sing unto the LORD, O ye saints of his, and give thanks at the remembrance of his holiness.

LORD, by thy favour thou hast made my mountain to stand strong: thou didst hide thy face, and I was troubled.

I cried to thee, O LORD; and unto the LORD I made supplication.

Thou hast turned for me my mourning into dancing: thou hast put off my sackcloth, and girded me with gladness;

To the end that my glory may sing praise to thee, and not be silent. O LORD my God, I will give thanks unto thee forever.
— Psalm 30:1-4, 7-8, 11-12

After the surgery, I woke up in the recovery room and looked over to my right and saw my wife. I reached over with my left hand and squeezed her hand, and she knew that I knew her. What we didn't know is that I could not talk and was paralyzed on my right side. The surgery lasted longer than they thought it would and I was not responding the way they had hoped. I would have to relearn to walk, talk, and do everyday things that people take for granted.

In the midst of all of this, I am a huge St. Louis Cardinals fan and they were in the World Series. I was in ICU watching games 6 and 7, and when they won, I tried to scream and all that came out was a weak little 'yea!" I tried to raise both arms and would throw my paralyzed right arm up and it would fall down. I also accidentally hit the nurse call button and the nurses came in and I very slowly said, "The Cardinals won the World Series!" That gives an idea of how at peace I was, in the midst of all of this.

About a week after surgery, the doctors decided that they were going to have me rehab in the Drake Center. Progress was slow, but I was making progress. I could talk in broken sentences. I began to gain feeling back in my right leg and arm. One of the first things that I asked the surgeon was "When could I go back to teaching?" Dr. Z said to not think about that and that the recovery could be long to the point that the springtime was maybe the best timeframe. I basically said, "Want to bet?"

Once again, there was that "peace that transcends all understanding". On November 4, I felt bold enough that I called the school when I knew my AP class was in the room and asked to speak to them. When they put me on speaker phone, I barely could get the words out "see... you....soon." It was then that I truly knew that it was going to be a long road to recover. I was broken, angry, and devastated all at the same time. I had to go back to the Word. The Word of God is truth and that truth is what we need to get through these crises in life!

> *And not only that, but we also glory in tribulations, knowing that tribulation produces perseverance; and perseverance, character; and character, hope. Now hope does not disappoint, because the love of God has been poured out in our hearts by the Holy Spirit who was given to us.* — Romans 5:3-5 NKJV

As mentioned before, the timeline for recovery was Spring Break for when I could go back to work. I left the Drake Center to go home to do outpatient rehab on November 11. Around that time, I had a follow up MRI and they found that there was still a piece of tumor embedded in my brain. The tumor was benign, and the doctors were debating whether to do radiation treatments or to let it go and watch the tumor. I did outpatient therapy and before Christmas, I went back to work half days. Not only that, I had a British accent and I teach AP European History! When I would come home each day, I was so worn out that I had to go into a dark room and lay down for a while. I would end up taking a driving test in mid-January and going back full time to work around that time. In the midst of all of this, my wife became pregnant and had a miscarriage. In the midst of the joy of being back to work, there was another roadblock of heartache.

In early March, I began to get headaches and feel symptoms again. So, I went in for an MRI. When I saw my oncologist soon after, she said, "Well, I can't explain it, but that remaining tumor is not there." My response was "God healed me in the name of Jesus!" There was no medical explanation for this. It was a miracle! Every MRI that I have had since has been clear! When the weather changes, I can still feel symptoms, but I've just learned that is scar tissue.

Throughout this whole time, the Hamilton High School community went through a lot. We had a student commit suicide early in the school year. Then, Duane Moore had a stint put in his heart and had almost died. Then, my brain tumor and situation happened. Then, Maribeth Robinson, an HHS principal, had a massive stroke and was unable to return to work. Over the summer in 2012, we had a teacher commit suicide. In the midst of all of this sorrow and heartache, there was peace that surpasses all understanding. There was hope in the midst of the chaos. On October 30, 2012, our 3rd little miracle was born, one year and 5 days after my neurosurgery. We named her Abigail (which means "the Father's Joy") Hope (the hope we have in the storms of life in Christ). There was light illuminating the darkness and there was a peace that was with us and calmed the storm. That hope and peace was Jesus Christ, who gave us the Holy Spirit to live inside of us each day.

CHAPTER EIGHT

One Woman's Loss and Heaven's Gain

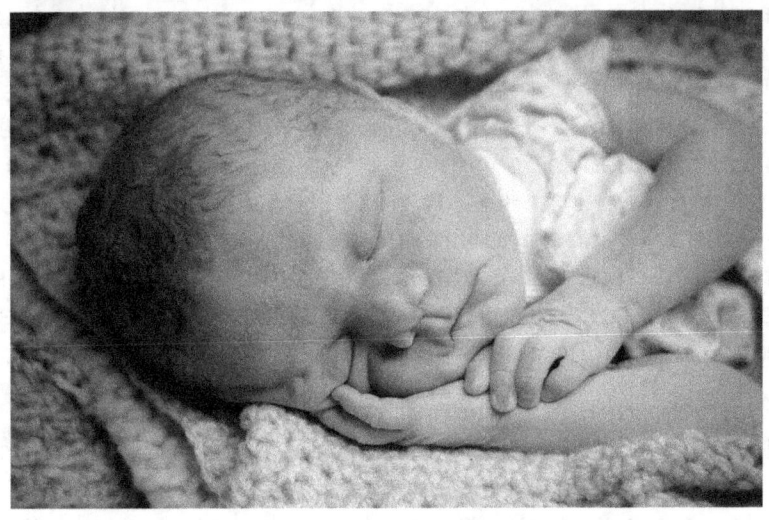

Owen Timothy Mann

ERIN TUNNAT MANN'S TESTIMONY

I had a memory recently of when I was a little girl, sitting on my parents' bed. I had just skinned my knee, and I was crying. My mother had some sort of antiseptic--camphophenique, I think it was called--it smelled awful. And she said to me, "this is going to burn, but it's important to clean your wound. We have to do this." My parents and sister were all there around me, and we were all ready; at the count of three, my mother applied the antiseptic and everyone blew on the wound. Like blowing on hot soup, the cool air helps the burning sensation go away. Grief is a lot like that. Getting wounded hurts. The healing process hurts. But being surrounded by loved ones, determined to go through it with you, makes the pain bearable.

The pain I would later go through with the loss of my baby is far beyond all the skinned knees and burning antiseptics. It's hard to imagine the pain that comes from losing a child. It's like your world shatters into such tiny shards of glass that you could never even imagine gluing back together. Your future, the future you imagined, the future that included that little person, will never be what you had pictured. It means you will be missing something, someone, forever. Even if all the shards of glass are glued together, the cracks will always remain.

We had not been exactly trying to conceive when Owen was created. My high-school-sweetheart husband, Andy, and I already had three wonderful kids and very busy lives. Our third baby had come into the world with drama; I developed pre-eclampsia, delivered her at 37 weeks, and lost quite a bit of blood at her delivery. For years after her birth, we assumed there would be no more children--my husband especially didn't want to risk my health. But when she was about three, I began to wonder if saying no to more children was the best thing for us. At a weekend at Grateful Heart Ministry's retreat house, I wondered out loud once again to Andy if we should take another shot at pregnancy. To my utter shock, this time he said, "Maybe we should."

Fast forward through many months of prayer and indecision, we decided not to try to conceive just yet but were going to be more open to conception. Natural Family Planning (NFP) was something I felt called to use, but I hadn't because I suspected we wouldn't do it correctly. Now that we were more open to failure, we decided to give NFP a try. It was in our first month of NFP that Owen was conceived.

While technically a failure, we were overjoyed. We wondered how my health would fare but decided to trust God and trust modern medicine to get us through. We loved how all the children were excited to have another baby. My oldest daughter, who was 11, was a veteran big sister by now and well-versed in the routines and needs of helping mom. My 8-year-old son was ready to have another boy in the family to rough-house with and play boyish games. Bethany, our little 3-year-old, was eager to be a big sister and claimed she would even change diapers.

Owen was such an active boy--I felt his movements at 10 weeks gestation. For those that don't know, that's super early. I didn't feel my first child's movements until I was 19 weeks. We got to know Owen through his movements. He loved when I took baths; he kicked when his siblings blew raspberries on my belly; and he woke up when he heard voices of his family members, especially when Andy came home from work in the middle of the night.

During his 20 week ultrasound, he was constantly moving. The ultrasound technician had to pause and rewind the video to take measurements. The children and Andy were in the ultrasound room when the technician announced, "It's a boy!" and my son Caden said, "Are you sure?!" Owen looked healthy, and everything was going well. My blood pressure continued to look healthy as the pregnancy went along. We decided on the name Owen Timothy. Owen, which meant "well-born" and "a noble warrior." Timothy was in honor of Andy's beloved Uncle Tim, who had been the officiant at our wedding, who had recently died after a long battle with cancer.

I struggled in the third trimester with depression and anxiety. I was taking medicine for both, just as I always had, even through my other pregnancies. This time it wasn't cutting it, but I didn't want to go higher on my dose. I tried to be gentle with myself and take it easy. I tried to focus on the end goal--my due date, delivery, meeting my little boy. I tried not to stress about things that weren't perfect, tried to keep expectations minimal in my life and my business. The due date slowly, ever-so-slowly, crept closer. It seemed as if I would be pregnant forever.

I knew, as active as he was inside me, that he would be an active baby and would surely be eager to catch up to his siblings. I imagined him popping out in the delivery room with his placenta under his arm like a football, sprinting past the nurses and running down the hospital halls. You could just tell: Owen couldn't wait to be a part of this world.

It was his familiar acrobatics that I had come to know and expect. Sometimes it gave me heartburn, and occasionally he got me right in the bladder, but it was just a part of being pregnant with Owen. One morning, the day before we hit 36 weeks, I woke up, and Owen didn't wake up with me. I tried a bath first, but he didn't respond. I asked Andy and the kids to come and talk to him, but he remained still. I even held a glass of ice water against my belly, knowing he would soon feel the cold through my skin, but he didn't reposition.

We drove to the doctor and I sent text messages to friends and family to pray. I told myself it was just a fluke. He was running out of room to move, that's all. The nurse put me into the ultrasound room, the same dark room we had all been in together during his 20-week scan, when we--all together--found out he was a boy. At first, I was alone. This was just a fluke; I wouldn't need any support for a fluke. I was going to receive good news! But as I sat there, I felt the truth settle on my shoulders. I would need Andy. We homeschool, so the kids and Andy were together, even though it was 10:45 on a Tuesday morning. I asked them all to come to the ultrasound room. The doctor arrived soon after and the machine turned on. On the screen, where we had seen such a flurry of activity before, was now just a gray stillness. There was such a quiet numbness to it. Even though I knew Owen wasn't moving, seeing the lack of motion on the screen was jarring to me. I held my breath. I could feel it coming. "I'm so sorry," the doctor said. I squeezed Andy's hand as I tried to suppress the tears.

It was in that moment that a memory from just the night before occurred to me. I had been waddling through the living room when Owen gave me a powerful kick. I had lamented out loud in my crampy, bloated, pregnant misery, "Oh I just want this to be OVER!" Even though I didn't mean for it to end like this, the fact that I had said that to Owen on his last night alive ripped through me. Every complaint I had uttered, I wished to take back. Oh, what more I would have endured if it meant I could have kept him! Every discomfort and pain I had endured paled in comparison to the pain I felt now.

The drive home was a blur. I remember texting family and friends:

"We lost Owen. Please pray." To my church friends I requested that they contact our priests and to "Call Donna." Donna was a friend of many of the women in my church community, a member of our women's bible study, and we all knew of Donna's ministry: Heaven's Gain. After three of her own losses, she began a ministry that serves families before, during, and after miscarriage, stillbirth, and infant loss. I had supported her ministry for years but never expected to need her. My church friends knew who I meant, so that's all I had to say. Our daughters cried. Our son asked what happened--why did Owen die, to which we had few answers: "These things happen. We know that Owen is with Jesus now, and that God loves us and Owen very much, and that God had a plan for us, and we have to Trust Him." Our youngest, who had just turned four, cried the most. It was hard to know if she truly comprehended what was happening, or just saw that we were upset and cried out of sympathy, but either way, I hated how disappointed she was. She had been so excited to be a big sister.

As we pulled into the driveway, Donna called, and as we spoke, I walked around my garden. One of my favorite flowers, my peonies, were all very close to blooming. I had been watching them and expecting them to bloom a few days later, but here, one had opened earlier than the rest. I picked it and looked at it while Donna comforted me and we made plans to meet. Later, I walked inside the house and said, "I think Owen made this one bloom early for me," and I put it in a vase. I hugged Andy and sobbed.

While I had talked to Donna, Andy made plans for our children to be cared for by grandparents for the day. Our doctor had told us to go to the hospital to have a confirmation ultrasound, a second pair of eyes to confirm Owen was gone. I don't know this, but I suspect it was also to get a clearer picture as to what he had died from, what position he was in, how large he was, and other details that would be helpful for the doctor to know as we approached delivery. Somehow the doctor's order for the ultrasound never arrived, so we sat in the main entrance of the hospital, facing the gift shop, for almost an hour. I looked at the little stuffed animal bears and balloons in the gift shop, and the nurses laughing and gossiping light-heartedly on their way to lunch. Each piece of light and hope that belonged in the happy hospital triage that would deliver many healthy, happy babies each day, felt like another stab on my wounded heart. We went to the desk a few times, asking what was taking so long. Eventually I eeked out the words, "We're here for an ultrasound to confirm our baby is dead. Do we really need an order from the doctor? Can't you just do it and get the order later?" While they were sympathetic, they were unwavering. Finally, I said to Andy that I couldn't take it any longer, and we walked out.

As we drove across town to meet with Donna at Heaven's Gain, I recall how my head, especially my face, ached and pounded like it never had before--looking back I think it was from suppressing my tears. I was miserable physically and mentally. Never had I wanted to escape this world like I did then. Donna hugged me when we arrived, and her "I'm so sorry" held the meaning of a veteran of loss. She knew the pain we felt. But here she sat, not shying away from the pain we were going through, but experiencing it with us, living it with us. She gave us wisdom that would prove to guide us in our path to healing.

She first told us that grief is the cost we pay for love. You can't throw out the grief without throwing the love away also. Grieving hurts, but it's important, and you can't skip over it. Owen deserved to be loved, and so he deserved to be grieved. He deserved to be remembered.

She told us that we had a precious opportunity to make memories with our boy while we had his body. She encouraged us to think of the things we wanted to do while we had him in our arms. This helped us think of things we would otherwise not have thought of and would have missed out on. Would we want to bathe him? Dance with him? Rock him in a chair? Read stories or sing lullabies?

She prepared us for what the delivery would look like, what Owen would look like, how big he would be, how much he would weigh, how his skin might look gray, how his body would be limp, how he might have damage to his wrinkly skin. She encouraged us not to rush into delivery, but to go home and rest.

Lastly, she told me something I had been desperate for someone to say out loud: our baby was in heaven. Theologically speaking, there was no doubt. I didn't need to worry or wonder where his soul was; it was safe in heaven. She reminded us that every soul that makes it to heaven is a saint, so our son was officially a saint and therefore a powerful intercessor for our family. He would spend eternity loved and held and happy, and whenever we called up on him to pray for us, he would do it with love. She reminded us that every item that touched our baby, every blanket, every wash cloth, every hat was truly a second-class relic of a saint, and that if he was born with hair, a lock of it would be a first-class relic. In Catholicism, Saintly relics bring us grace by orienting our hearts toward heaven; they bestow grace not of their own, but of Christ. Nevertheless, they are special and connect us in a physical way to the heavenly realm. She talked about how her own losses had given her a stronger desire for heaven; she not only would meet her heavenly father, but she would also meet her sons as well.

I've been questioned by Protestants about this Catholic belief about relics and praying "to" saints. I hope you'll allow me to clarify-- Catholics believe that the saints in heaven can hear our prayers and that they can pray for us, and with us, to God. They exist in a realm that has no barrier between them and God; they are face-to-face with the Almighty Creator. We don't need saints to pray for us; we don't need Mary to pray for us; but why would we not want a heavenly advocate joining us in prayer to the Father that we share? Sacred relics are not powerful in and of themselves, but they can be vessels of grace. Just as the hemorrhaging woman needed to just touch the cloak of Jesus to be healed, and Jesus said to her, "Your FAITH has healed you," so too is our FAITH that makes relics holy and special. A relic is meant to deliver grace from God the Father, not from the Saint. It is to orient us to heaven, to our Savior, not to the Saint. They are physical representations, connections, to heaven. They are not a replacement for prayer.

Speaking of prayer, our friends and families rallied prayer chains and prayer vigils. As the grief surrounded us, I knew we were held in prayer. One friend said she would pray for Mary to be at my shoulders and for Jesus to be with the doctor, ready to catch Owen as he left my womb. Another friend was traveling and just happened to be visiting the shrine of Saint Philomena, the patron saint of infants. She asked Saint Philomena to pray for Owen and for us. There were friends at our church that signed up to pray for us each hour of the day that we delivered Owen. The day was solemn, but I felt strengthened by the multitude of prayers and the comfort and peace of a loving Father.

BITTER TO BETTER

I worried that Andy's faith, never really all that strong to begin with, would not be able to withstand this storm. I told my mother, "Pray that Andy does not forsake God over this." This prayer was answered: Andy was a rock and held my hand throughout. He was always there when I needed a hug. I never felt alone.

The next day as we walked into the hospital at 8 am, there was an announcement over the PA system; it was time for the morning prayer over the entire hospital. The announcer prayed over all the people they would serve today. It was a comforting feeling, knowing I was in a hospital that prayed. As we walked to my room, pictures on the walls of the maternity ward showed babies and their happy mothers, and I felt the pain of the contrast in my core. However, I was treated with utmost gentleness and kindness. I saw no other mothers, nor heard them. I felt like the only mother in the maternity ward that day. We discussed our birth plan and began the induction.

The labor was hardly difficult physically; they gave me an epidural and I felt comfortable and well-cared for. While we waited, Andy and I watched a favorite funny movie ("Fletch") knowing that it might not ever be funny for us again after this, but that we needed something light-hearted to pass the time. When it came time to push, the room was dim, quiet, and reverent. Even the nurses' encouragements to push were whispers. When Owen came out, Andy stole a glance at his body and said to me, "He's perfect," but his voice was hardly audible through his suppressed sob. The nurses wrapped Owen in a blanket, handed him to us, and left us alone to slowly meet our boy. Andy was right; he was perfect. He had an adorable chin and soft ears. Other than the gray hue to his skin and his black lips, he looked like a baby that was asleep.

The delivery day, the day I had waited for for what seemed like forever. The moment, holding him in my arms at last. There was a feeling in my chest, like a void, a black hole. I put him to my chest but the void didn't feel filled. His body was there, but there was no feeling of union that you are so used to feeling when you hug a person. This emptiness in my chest hurt most of all. It would not go away for several months.

Our family joined us; Owen's siblings and grandparents filled the room. The sun shone as we made our memories with Owen. Favorite stories were read, songs were sung. I did "this little piggie went to the market" on his tiny toes. Grandparents rocked him in the rocking chair. We took many pictures and cried many tears. We bathed him with a special soap that smelled like baptism chrism, and with his vernix washed away, his skin was more pink than gray. He looked even more alive than before. We made momentos of his hand and footprints. As evening fell, our priest came and baptized Owen and commended him to heaven. Our four-year-old, who had been shy of Owen's body all day, finally warmed up to him. It gave my mama heart peace to know she got a chance to hold him like a big sister would.

A week later, we had a funeral and burial. Heaven's Gain provided a beautiful baby casket, which brought me comfort knowing his body was honored. The funeral home offered, by contrast, a plastic "vault" that reminded me of a cooler you'd put your beers in for a picnic. The funeral home advisor, while well-meaning, was definitely out of touch. Many people came to the visitation. They got to see Owen, although he looked so very different than he had just a week ago. It felt right to honor his life, and our loss, the way we would if he had been born alive and then died. The kids put little gifts into his coffin with him. When we closed the coffin for the last time, I felt crushed like a tin can. But inside, I knew, even if I could hold him again, it wouldn't help. Holding him didn't soothe the empty feeling in my chest, and it never would. My maternal instinct was to bring his little body to my protective heart, but I was disappointed each time. I was reminded of the angels at Jesus' tomb upon the resurrection; "He is not here." I couldn't stay by the grave when he was lowered into the ground. As we drove away, I thought about how the chapter was finally finished. The hardest part was over. I had survived thus far. I would survive the rest. Our time with Owen had ended. We had squeezed out all the memories that we could. We could rest knowing we had done all that we could.

These memories were hard to make. And for a while, they were hard to remember. But over time, they had less pain and more beauty. Our time with Owen was a gift, and it was cherished. We had an album made of the pictures taken of me during our pregnancy and all the pictures taken during his day with us, and even of him in his coffin, with all the makeup that made him look like a different baby. This album now holds a place of honor in our living room, right above the piano. I saved other mementos of him: his "coming home from the hospital" outfit that he briefly wore; his hospital hat; the blanket that our oldest had knitted for him; his hospital bracelet; and tiny footprints. All were put into a shadow-box that hangs in our upstairs hallway, in between the doorways to our other children's rooms. Sometimes, at night, when I tuck in our other children, I walk by the shadow-box and say goodnight to Owen, too. He is mentioned every night in our nightly prayers: "Thank you Jesus, for Mommy and Daddy, Lydia and Caden, Bethany and Owen; for all the people we know, and all the people we don't know. May they be safe and happy and healthy and know Your love. Saint Owen, pray for us." We have made sure that Owen never stopped being a part of our family.

Since then I have heard about so many people who had not been given the wisdom that made such a difference to us. Well-meaning doctors often encourage parents not to see or hold their dead babies, because it would cause pain. But the pain is necessary. It is part of love. It is part of grief. I can tell you with confidence that I am grateful for the pain.

Fortunately, Andy did not turn away from God. He remained a rock and turned toward God for strength. His faith grew, rather than faltered, and mine did the same. Someone once asked me, "How can you not be mad at God?" and I responded, "God did not take my boy from me. He saved him. It is because of Jesus's sacrifice that I will get to meet Owen one day."

I missed Owen the most during Mass. Our faith teaches us that heaven and earth both participate in the Mass; that the space between heaven and earth is thinnest during the Mass; that when we sing, "Holy Holy Holy" to God, the saints and angels sing with us. Through the Eucharist, we are in communion with all the members of the body of Christ, including Owen. Owen was not at the grave, but he was here in this church, sharing this space where our realms touched. Knowing that his spirit was so near, but that he wasn't in my arms, hurt for many weeks. I thought of how I would have rocked and bounced him during the service; how he would not get to meet all our church friends; and how he would not coo and cry and disrupt Mass like all children do, earning the sympathetic and happy glances of the people that are not the least upset to be distracted by something so adorable.

The pain of losing Owen never goes away but ebbs and flows. Milestones and holidays hurt most because it's obvious that what I expected those days to look like is not what they are. That's the thing about losing someone; you never expect them not to be there until they aren't. The world is just a tiny bit darker than you had expected it to be.

One thing that got me through the darkest moments of grief, and I don't recall coming up with this on my own, but I repeated to myself when I felt like falling apart: "I made a baby for heaven. I made a baby for heaven." It helped, I guess, to consider my work of growing him still of value; it wasn't wasted. I didn't bury in the ground the person I grew in my womb; I commended him to his Heavenly father. In all the places in the world for me to want my child, heaven is the place of ultimate happiness, joy, and peace. Other than my own loss of not knowing him in this life, how can I be sad for him? He will never know hunger. He will never skin his knee. He will never lose a game of baseball or get his heart broken by the wrong girl. His life, his existence, has been and always will be love and love alone. I imagine him being passed around the angels and saints cooing over him, teaching him to crawl or walk. Is he aging at the same pace he would on earth? Is his soul already a man? It doesn't truly matter. What matters is that he is enveloped in the loving arms of his Almighty Creator. My wise oldest daughter told me, "Your goal as a mother is to get all your children into heaven. With Owen, you have already succeeded!"

I could have blamed God. I could have lashed out, but I know that God didn't take Owen from me. No one on this earth is guaranteed tomorrow, nor are they entitled to it. We are all on loan from heaven. Each day alive with the people we love is a gift.

As I write this, it has not yet been a year since his death. Memories of my baby bump mirror selfies still show up on Facebook. I remember how I felt taking those selfies; how I thought I was getting so big; how heavy my belly had become; and how it felt like my due date would never arrive. I look forward at my life and see my death as my new due date: the day I get to meet my boy. My day to hold my boy against my chest and truly feel him, that day is still going to happen. It is just delayed.

BITTER TO BETTER

Grief is not what God had in mind for any of us. Pain, death--these are the result of sin, not God's design. In my darkest moments, I did not feel bitter because I could feel the Spirit surrounding and embracing me. I knew that God wept with me. I knew then, and know now, that it is God's mercy and sacrifice that pave the way for my reunion with Owen. I can march forward, my eyes on the prize, because I know I am loved, deeply loved. God did not do this to me. God gives me the second chance I don't deserve to get to hold my boy. The reunion I joyfully await is not just the union of mother and child, but of Creator and Created. God desires to hold me to his chest just as much, if not more, than I desire to hold my Owen. I can never fault my Heavenly Father for the pain of my grief, because grief is just the other side of a great love, a love that comes from God; a love that God first gave me. Owen was a gift. I just don't get to unwrap that gift fully until I reach heaven. The light that has been missing from my world burns on in heaven, and that reunion, I am sure, will be brighter than I could ever imagine. At Owen's funeral, the closing song was "How Can I Keep from Singing" and we chose that on purpose. Our story is a sad one, but it has a happy ending; not because we deserve it, but because God loves us so very much. The love I feel for Owen, the desire to hold him against my chest and kiss his face, pales in comparison to the love God feels for each of us.

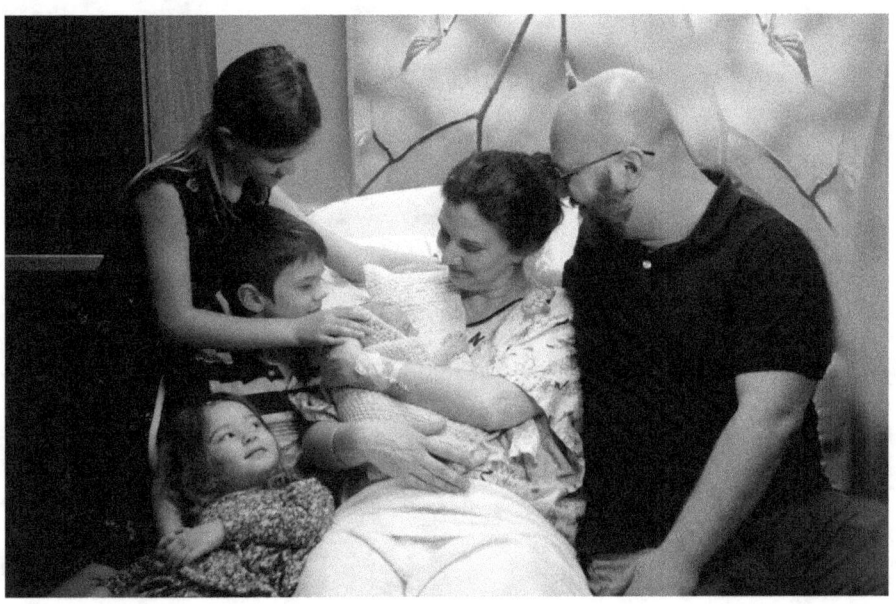

Erin and her family

CHAPTER NINE

Concluding the Pottery Story

THE REST OF THE POTTERY STORY

No one wants to experience bitterness, loss, or disappointment, but when we work through the experience, we can learn so much about ourselves and about other people. Taking a clinical approach to a bitter situation, we can analyze how it happened, how we responded, how others responded, and what we could have done differently.

Thinking about what prompted our emotions and what prompted the emotions or responses of others, we can guide ourselves back through the event or series of events using a different approach. We can analyze the dynamics of the people involved, the setting, the circumstances, the timing, our emotional state, others' emotional states, and what was happening all around us. And then....we add GRACE to the scenario. What if we gave GRACE to others and to ourselves, just as God gives us grace all the time?

Even though bitterness is not fun or desirable, the experience can teach us about what is important to us, what is important to others, and how we can develop more empathy for others. Often when we rerun the bitter film in our minds and hearts, we get the same negative responses. However, what if we tried to play the role of others to see what they may have been feeling, thinking, or doing that played a part in our feelings of bitterness? Did they act intentionally, shrewdly, competently, and with malice? Or were they unintentional, obtuse, incompetent, or victims themselves? Did they have control over our situation or theirs? Were they operating in a larger framework of control or generational cycle beyond what they could control themselves? Were they even aware that we were affected at all? Do they even know that we were bitter about their words or actions? This process helps us to determine the source of the bitterness and possible causes.

My husband, Darrell, is the most considerate person in my world. His approach to life is to think that people have the best possible intentions, until they prove otherwise. Whenever I talk with him about situations involving other people, he listens attentively. After some time of reflection, Darrell will ask questions or make comments that show me the other possibilities, perspectives, points of view or intentions. When I listen to him resolving issues with people in customer service, often he asks for clarification or considers what else another person may have been thinking or how he could have possibly misunderstood what he reads or hears people say. More often than not, his assumptions about people are correct. Typically, they mean well, even if their actions signal otherwise. More often than not, Darrell resolves issues with other people in the kindest of ways, and they seem to appreciate his approach. Everyone needs a "Darrell" to help balance our thinking, emotions, and responses.

Here is what I have learned from Darrell:

- Listen more attentively.
- Consider the speaker's point of view.
- Consider other possible interpretations in a situation.
- Reflect.
- Be kind.
- Give grace.
- Speak when the time is appropriate.
- Compromise when necessary or possible.
- Find peace with the process.
- Move on.

I started the introduction of this book with a metaphor of a potter's jar that had been broken and transformed into a beautiful mosaic work of art. I have always thought fondly about my relationship with God: he is the Potter, and I am the clay from the book of Isaiah.

Yet you, Lord, are our Father. We are the clay, you are the potter; we are all the work of your hand. — Isaiah 64:8

Recently I have meditated on Jeremiah 18 when God sent the prophet Jeremiah to a potter's house to watch how the potter works at his wheel to form a pot. When the potter was not satisfied with his creation and saw that it was marred, he re-formed it into the pot that seemed best to him.

This is the word that came to Jeremiah from the Lord: "Go down to the potter's house, and there I will give you my message." So

I went down to the potter's house, and I saw him working at the wheel. But the pot he was shaping from the clay was marred in his hands; so the potter formed it into another pot, shaping it as seemed best to him.

Then the word of the Lord came to me. He said, "Can I not do with you, Israel, as this potter does?" declares the Lord. "Like clay in the hand of the potter, so are you in my hand, Israel. If at any time I announce that a nation or kingdom is to be uprooted, torn down and destroyed, and if that nation I warned repents of its evil, then I will relent and not inflict on it the disaster I had planned. And if at another time I announce that a nation or kingdom is to be built up and planted, and if it does evil in my sight and does not obey me, then I will reconsider the good I had intended to do for it.
— Jeremiah 18:1-10

This Scripture took me back to Isaiah's description of us being the "work" of God's hands, this time making me think about us being a "work in progress" in our relationship with the Lord. In Jeremiah, God sends him to warn his people that they can be "uprooted, torn down, and destroyed" at his will, and that God "will reconsider the good" that he had intended.

On a recent trip to the western states, my husband and I saw many beautiful pieces of pottery hand crafted by Native Americans. I also admired pottery made by a local pastor and sold at a local art fair and peach festival. I was moved to purchase a couple of inexpensive pieces of her work. I asked her to sign it because I knew that she had "poured" herself into each piece. She was so joyful and took such joy in her work that it was contagious. I felt joyful just talking with her about her passion for pottery.

In the back of my mind, I was on the hunt for beautiful but broken pieces of pottery that I wanted to use as a demonstration in my next speaking engagement, possibly at a women's retreat. I thought that I could hold up the broken pieces and talk about the vision of God wanting to restore us or transform us through our brokenness into something even more beautiful and purposeful. I asked the pastor/potter if she had any broken pieces or knew where I could acquire any. She directed me to a pottery store that had a "Shatter Garden" displayed in front. The Shatter Garden was the place where potters' mistakes were broken and left to join all the other potters' first, second, and third attempts to create their best work.

From the art fair, we found our way to the pottery store, The Tilted Kiln, and saw the entire front of the store decorated with colorful broken pottery pieces instead of the typical botanical landscaping. I explained to the young girl at the front desk about our search for broken pottery pieces. She gave us permission to take some samples from their Shatter Garden and offered us a bag. Instead, we got some boxes from our truck and filled two of them with a wide variety of broken pieces with gorgeous glazes, interesting shapes, and a range of sizes. I didn't think about a limit because I knew that many more broken pieces would be added in the near future. After all, it was a pottery store where people were trying to make art from clay all day long, amateurs to professionals. There would be many more mistakes to come.

After we put the boxes in our truck, we toured the pottery store, watched people taking pottery lessons, and purchased several finished products displayed on the retail shelves. A potter, working on her next project, explained for us the meaning behind several vases. She stayed seated on the floor, unable to rise easily because of a broken ankle from a running accident. Her foot was in a brace, but she continued to prepare paints in jars and assemble her supplies. Under her broad brimmed felt hat, she had long, thick black hair, dark sparkly eyes, a decorative artist's scarf around her neck, a baggy plaid cotton shirt, and stone washed blue jeans. Her long delicate fingers moved quickly and gestured dramatically as she worked and spoke. We looked at all the pottery items on all the shelves and were mesmerized at the variety of creative genius displayed in one place. When we mentioned an article or two, she related the type of glaze or the artist's name or a particular significance attached.

We asked the potter which of hers was her favorite. She noted a black, textured, amorphous bottle or vase. Her creation was, indeed, a vase with a jet black coating and subdued sparkles for the finish or "glaze". It had indentations the size of a thumb or fingers around it. My husband, Darrell, carefully picked it up and mentioned the practicality of the vase with places to grab and not drop it. However, the potter clarified that the dents were not for practicality but for artistic interpretation. The stumpy vase's color was black as an ode to the surrounding lands of volcanic ash and black lava rocks in the nearby terrain where she lived and worked; the sparkles represented her attraction to the ashy soil that made up the trails where she ran and hiked; and the indentations signified that not all nature and humankind are perfectly formed, sometimes beautifully dented or given to outside pressures, but not purposely flawed. This beautiful black, subtly sparkly vase became Darrell's favorite piece of the whole pottery shop. It has a special place in our home today.

We purchased several other pieces and paid for these one-of-a-kind finds. As we checked out, instead of the young girl, an older man managed the register. We learned that he was the owner. As I thanked him for the pieces from the Shatter Garden, he seemed peculiarly concerned. He explained that the Shatter Garden was a special place for potters from the community to say goodbye lovingly to their flawed works and to give them a new purpose by joining other broken pieces. In their broken state, resting in peace as they create a new design, together they are transformed into a new work of art. He said that it is an almost spiritual action by the artists to let go of their mistakes and to let a piece of themselves "grieve" the loss before moving on to create other pieces freely.

Darrell and I had no idea that the Shatter Garden was so meaningful to the local artists. We had assumed that the shop owner had found an inexpensive way to landscape the front of his store to draw

attention to shoppers. I told him that we were given permission by the young blonde when we came in, and he explained that she was his granddaughter and not to worry. We could keep a couple of pieces, he surmised. We left the store, and I told Darrell that I was glad that the owner did not see just how many "dead bodies" of pottery that we had taken from his "cemetery" garden.

As we drove away, Darrell felt that we needed to return the "dead" to their "resting place", since it was so important to the store owner and the artists. I knew that he was right, but I so wanted to use the pottery pieces to demonstrate God's mercy and grace. I argued for a better use, but Darrell kindly and calmly argued for doing the right thing. The owner thought he had given us a "couple of pieces", not boxes of "bones" from his garden. Reluctantly but finally conceding to doing the right thing, we decided to return to the store to replace all of the pottery pieces back into the Shatter Garden.

I was embarrassed to show the store owner how much we took, albeit with his granddaughter's permission. We felt like grave robbers, so we worked quickly and stayed away from the front door and windows of the store. I took a few photos of the garden. At least I would be able to show the pictures to future audiences for some emotional effect. We jumped back in the truck and took off. I just couldn't face the owner, as if I had committed some sort of crime. I called him on the phone and explained that we had returned every piece to the Shatter Garden. I just didn't mention how many! He responded kindly, "Oh, you didn't have to do that, but I am so grateful that you did. This garden is a very special place to many of our craftsmen. It helps them to grieve their shattered dreams of their beautiful pieces, and it gives them peace."

I don't hope to understand that level of connection with a piece of broken pottery, but I do understand the level of connection that God keeps with us, no matter how broken or flawed or shattered we are, or how far from perfection we may be. I often think of that Shatter Garden. It has been captured in my emotional memory bank with the realization that I need to refrain from rationalizing my actions based upon what is good for me and mine and to focus on what is best for all.

Readers, you will just have to be content with picturing a colorful section of pottery pieces of all sizes, shapes, weights, and textures in the Shatter Garden to memorialize brokenness and loss. If you are still hanging on to bitterness or disappointment, I recommend that you create your own version of a Shatter Garden, say goodbye, grieve a bit, and then move on, knowing that your broken pieces have joined the millions of broken pieces left behind by others who have decided to move forward in their lives. We don't need to go back and pick them up, box them up, treasure them, or revisit them. Just know that all is well, and a space has been made for our bitterness to rest in pieces, and for our emotions to rest in peace. Choose strategies that lead you to a greater level of mental health and spiritual maturity.

To God be the glory!

CHAPTER TEN

My Present Reality of "Done Done!" in Revelation

WHAT FUELS MY BRAIN AND MY SOUL

After more than a year writing, studying, and collecting research and testimonies about the transformation from being bitter to better, I have been sharing some of my collective information and passion for Scripture at speaking engagements. I read Dr. Caroline Leaf's book, "Switch On Your Brain" and use her devotional, "Switch On Your Brain Every Day". I highly recommend her books for those of us who need reminders, maybe even daily reminders, to be mindful of thinking positively and to refrain from slipping back into a bitter mentality.

I have also been studying and rereading the book of Revelation with intensity and self-reflection. Revelation is the New Testament bookend to the Old Testament history of God's covenant with his people and the confirmation of the second coming of Jesus Christ, our Savior who suffered, died, and resurrected to save us from our sins and to give us eternal life in heaven. In years past, while I have studied other books of the Bible intensely and have published devotionals for some, I had scurried through Revelation because of all the past sermons and videos of End Times. Not only did I not want to dwell on the End of the World, I also did not want to dread the end of my own life on Earth. I had come to view the book of Revelation as a negative, fear-inducing prophecy rather than a positive, hope-inducing message for those choosing righteousness and a life as Jesus followers.

Considering that our time on this earth is temporary and that God has heaven waiting for those who remain faithful, we can think of every situation as temporary. The bitter times in our lives will get better if we change how we view our challenges and difficulties, even if our circumstances never change. We can always look forward to a time when there will be no more death, no more tears...only joy in heaven with Jesus and all the saints who have gone before us!

Now I approach the book of Revelation recognizing the trio of adversaries as Satan, the AntiChrist, and the false prophets, and I can rejoice that they will be overpowered and defeated by the powerful Holy Trinity of God, Jesus, and Spirit. I have recognized the need for the three strategies of Christian living: worshiping God, reading the Truth in the Word of God (the Bible), and living a righteous life in community with Christian believers.

As I read Revelation, I take a personal interest in the warnings of Jesus to the seven churches as a way to put my spirit in check. I imagine the vision and the sounds and the wonder and awe as John received this amazing prophecy. What can we take from this vision and prophetic word that we can carry with us on a daily basis? I receive joy, hope, a sense of spiritual victory, a promise of Jesus' return, a drive to live a more righteous life, and God's commitment that he is our God and we are his people.

From beginning to end, the Bible proclaims God's covenant with us, God's promise to us: "I will be their God and they will be my people".

In a world of chaos, wars, senseless idolatry and debauchery, I can still remain joyful and hopeful, definitely not bitter, with the promise of Revelation: that God will restore broken Eden to a New Jerusalem. I can decide that I am going to face God and Jesus with the Holy Spirit at some point in the future, either at the point of my death or at the point of Jesus' Second Coming, whichever happens first. I am on a journey through life together with my fellow Christians and future Christians.

Revelation 3:19-20

Those whom I love I rebuke and discipline. So be earnest and repent. Here I am! I stand at the door and knock. If anyone hears my voice and opens the door, I will come in and eat with that person, and they with me.

On February 18, 2024, I received this Word from God at the altar after a Sunday service:

"My Word, the Bible, is your sword/my sword, my shield/your shield... learn how to use it better and faster and clearer and cleaner, then go and fight the dragon in my name, the name I will give you, and in the name of my son, Jesus, with courage, hope, faith, and great joy!!!! Dig in and go, make disciples of all nations!"

Revelation 12:11

They triumphed over him
  by the blood of the Lamb
and by the word of their testimony;
  they did not love their lives so much
as to shrink from death.

The Dragon (Satan) and accusers were defeated by the blood of the Lamb and BY THEIR TESTIMONY and they did not love their lives so much that they were afraid to die.

Revelation 12:17 Then the dragon was enraged at the woman and went off to wage war against the rest of her offspring—those who keep God's commands and hold fast their testimony about Jesus.

The Dragon was angry at the woman and declared war against the rest of her children-- all who keep God's commandments and MAINTAIN THEIR TESTIMONY FOR JESUS!

The only war in which I want to be a warrior is that of the spiritual warfare that exists daily in our lives: the war for our souls, the war for our thoughts (our brain health), and the war for our next generations. With Jesus as our Dragonslayer over Satan as the enemy of souls, we will see victory! Not only is Jesus "finished" with his prophetic role of crucifixion, resurrection, and ascension into heaven; but God also proclaims the reality of his completion of his redemption of souls in Revelation with his New Jerusalem, his re-creation of a new heaven and earth.

John 19:28-30 (WHERE JESUS' SACRIFICE HAS BEEN PAID)
Later, knowing that everything had now been finished, and so that Scripture would be fulfilled, Jesus said, "I am thirsty." A jar of wine vinegar was there, so they soaked a sponge in it, put the sponge on a stalk of the hyssop plant, and lifted it to Jesus' lips. When he had received the drink, Jesus said, "It is finished." With that, he bowed his head and gave up his spirit.When he had received the drink, Jesus said, "It is finished. "With that, he bowed his head and gave up his spirit.

Revelation 16:17 (GOD'S FINAL WRATH PAID TO THE UNREPENTANT EARTH)
The seventh angel poured out his bowl into the air, and out of the temple came a loud voice from the throne, saying, "It is done!"

Revelation 21:1-7 (WHERE IT ENDS AND BEGINS ANEW IN HEAVEN)
Then I saw "a new heaven and a new earth," for the first heaven and the first earth had passed away, and there was no longer any sea. I saw the Holy City, the new Jerusalem, coming down out of heaven from God, prepared as a bride beautifully dressed for her

husband. And I heard a loud voice from the throne saying, "Look! God's dwelling place is now among the people, and he will dwell with them. They will be his people, and God himself will be with them and be their God. 'He will wipe every tear from their eyes. There will be no more death' or mourning or crying or pain, for the old order of things has passed away."

He who was seated on the throne said, "I am making everything new!" Then he said, "Write this down, for these words are trustworthy and true."

He said to me: "It is done. I am the Alpha and the Omega, the Beginning and the End. To the thirsty I will give water without cost from the spring of the water of life. Those who are victorious will inherit all this, and I will be their God and they will be my children.

The great voice proclaims, in essence in modern urban vernacular, that God is "done done" with his judgment and his creation. **"Done done"** is an expression of total completion that I learned from my teen granddaughters, Madelyn and Remy. Urbandictionary.com defines this expression as "a phrase to say when one has finished something that was so involved that it is as though one has done it twice."

Now, with the help of Strong's Greek lexicons, let's get formally theological considering the difference between the words "finish" and "done":

In John 19, Jesus on the cross cried out, "It is finished!" The Greek word here for "finished" is the adjective the**ΤΕΤΕΛΕΣΤΑΙ**, tetelestai, meaning "it has been accomplished, paid in full, fulfilled." Jesus described his action of dying on the cross as the fulfillment of his role as sacrificial Lamb, as prophesied.

In Revelation 16, the voice proclaiming the seventh and final bowl of wrath on the earth says, "It is done!" The Greek word here for "finished/done", is ΓΕΓΟΝΑΝ, gegonan, meaning "it has come into being" or "it is happening", that is, "transitioning from one state of being to another." The voice from the throne regarding the bowl of wrath describes the beginning of the end of the old earth.

In Revelation 21, the great voice of God declares the new heaven and earth, **"It is done."** The same Greek word here for **"done"** is the noun ΓΕΓΟΝΑΝ, gegonan, meaning "it has come into being." The words from the great voice of God proclaims the completion of the action of fulfillment. It is an event, a final completion of his creation or his re-creation.

What a subtle but powerful stamp of completion of God's covenant of redemption for his people! All created human beings will have exercised their free will to be for or against their Creator; all of God's judgment will have been administered to all human beings; and the past, present, and future will be consolidated into one present span of eternity.

Jesus was "done" with his sacrifice, God will be "done" with the seventh angel of wrath completing God's judgment of the earth, and God will be "done done" with his creations when Jesus returns.

As Jesus tells John in the final chapter of the final book of the Bible:

Revelation 22:12-13—

Look, I am coming soon! My reward is with me, and I will give to each person according to what they have done. I am the Alpha and the Omega, the First and the Last, the Beginning and the End.

The choice is ours; the final judgment is God's; and the reward is Jesus. Choose today whom you will serve. Choose today to be made well, whole, and holy in the sight of God. Healthy choices today lead to external rewards tomorrow.

In the first chapter of Genesis, as God was creating the earth, he said, "Let there be light."

Now the earth was formless and empty, darkness was over the surface of the deep, and the Spirit of God was hovering over the waters.

And God said, "Let there be light," and there was light. God saw that the light was good, and he separated the light from the darkness.

In Revelation 21 when Jesus returns, there will be no more need for earth's light, for the glory of God will be our light, and Jesus will be our lamp through which God's light will shine upon us.

The city does not need the sun or the moon to shine on it, for the glory of God gives it light, and the Lamb is its lamp.
—Revelation 21:23

Let us walk in His light, leaving behind any bitterness and choosing to be made well, to be made whole. Shalom!

CLOSING PRAYER

Lord God,

We give you all the praise, honor, and glory for who you are. You are the Alpha and Omega, the First and the Last. We praise you for your powerful yet gentle Holy Spirit.

We thank you for your Son, Jesus Christ, who died on the cross to save us from our sins and sinful natures. We are in awe of your everlasting grace and mercy, your compassion on us, your enduring patience toward the saved and unsaved.

We want to join the angels and saints in praising you around your throne in heaven, and we seek to lead a righteous life toward that end of spending eternity with you.

We thank you for your holy Word that speaks truth and faithfulness. We honor you for your eternal covenant to be our God and for us to be your people.

Come and dwell within our hearts and purify our souls so that we can be unified in your spirit and love.

We are forever grateful that you have created us, that you have instructed us, and that you have guided us to live each day with eyes to see, ears to hear, and hearts to feel your majesty, mercy, and greatness.

There is no one like you. May you be glorified and honored by all that we say and do. May we be made whole and holy in your sight! Until Jesus comes again, we say and sing, "Hallelujah! Amen! Come, Lord Jesus. Come!"

AFTERWORD
REV. DR. BONNIE NEWELL

"Do you want to be made well?" —John 5:6

"Get up! Pick up your mat and walk." —John 5:8

BITTER TO BETTER

The daffodil plants in my yard had not bloomed in two years. They grew tall green leaves but no flowers, so I decided to get rid of them. I pulled on the leaves and they snapped off at ground level. Perfect, no more green leaves cluttering my landscaping. A few weeks later, I noticed the leaves were growing back. Since the root was still in the ground, the plant grew again. I had to completely dig up the root for the plant to be permanently gone from my yard. Digging up the root took much more effort than merely snapping the leaves.

Bitterness is like those daffodil plants. If you only snap off the bitterness, it looks good to the people around you, but if you keep the root in your heart, the bitterness regrows. It is worth the extra effort to dig up the root of bitterness from your heart rather than risk it growing back again and again.

Unforgiveness is often the cause of bitterness that can control your life. A dear friend of mine had tragic events happen in her life. She and her husband lost a daughter to a congenital heart disease in early adulthood. She knew their son-in-law was unfaithful to their daughter while she was seriously ill. Some years later, the ex-boyfriend of their youngest daughter murdered her and killed himself in their home. Do you think she had valid reasons to be bitter? How would you respond to tragic events like these? Many say, "Forgive and forget." My friend said, "You must forgive every time you remember." Forgiving and rooting out bitterness is important, but the hurt may resurface in your mind from time to time. That's when it is time to forgive–every time you remember.

I've heard it said that when bitterness controls your life, it's like taking poison and waiting for the other person to die. Bitterness only hurts you, not the other person. The premier question in the book is, "Do you want to be made well?" Only you can answer this question. Only you can take the first step in the journey to root out unforgiveness and bitterness and press forward to wholeness.

The journey won't be easy, but God promises He will walk with you every step of the way. "The Lord himself goes before you; he will never leave you nor forsake you. Do not be afraid; do not be discouraged (Deuteronomy 31:7-8)." What do you need to do to take the first step today? — Rev. Dr. Bonnie Newell

APPENDIX 1

Brain Health Research

LIFE COACHING
& Consulting Associates

RELAXATION TECHNIQUES

By using the relaxation resources below, you will gain better control over the stress and anxiety.

DEEP DIAPHRAGMATIC BREATHING is a very effective, yet simple method for overcoming stress; one that can be done anywhere, anytime! Taking deep breaths relaxes your muscles, relieves tension, and helps your brain function better.

When you're feeling anxious or angry, your breathing becomes shallow and fast. This causes a change in oxygen in your blood (oxygen decreases while carbon dioxide increases), making you more anxious. Slight changes in oxygen content in the brain can alter the way a person feels and behaves. It becomes a vicious cycle, causing irritability, impulsiveness, confusion, and bad decision-making.

Learning to direct and control your breathing has immediate benefits. It calms the brain's amygdala (the brain's fear centers), counteracts the body's stress response, relaxes muscles, warms hands, and regulates heart rhythms. This simple diaphragmatic breathing exercise can help calm you almost immediately.

To practice breathing from your diaphragm, try this:

1. Lie on your back and place a small book on your belly.

2. As you slowly inhale through your nose, make the book go up. Hold your breath at the top of your inhalation for 3 seconds.

3. Hold for 1 second.

4. When you exhale, make the book go down and exhale for 6 seconds (twice as long as inhale).

5. Hold for 1 second.

6. Repeat 10 times and notice how relaxed you feel.

HAVENING

Havening is a very simple strategy you can use to calm yourself and wash away anxiousness or anger. It stimulates both sides of the brain and creates calming brain waves in the emotional centers of the brain.

Practice havening whenever you're upset, stressed, or anxious.

1. Cross your arms and put each hand on the opposite shoulder.

2. Gently stroke down.

3. While you're stroking down, say, "I am safe, I am here, this is now."

4. Repeat for 30-60 seconds.

HAND WARMING is a very helpful technique used to create generalized relaxation throughout your brain and body.

Whenever you are stressed or anxious, your hands get cold because your brain diverts the blood from your hands and feet to the large muscles in your body so that you can be ready to fight or run. Learning to warm your hands with your brain helps to counteract this automatic stress response.

Here's how to warm your hands using your brain:

1. Close your eyes and hold your hands out, palms down, and visualize (a campfire in front of you).

2. Focus. Think heat. You can hear the fire crackle, smell the aroma of fresh-cut wood burning, watch sparks fly and float up into the sky.

3. Now feel the soothing heat as it penetrates the surface of your skin and goes deep to warm your hands.

4. Picture this as you breathe deeply and count slowly to 20.

Potential Hand-Warming Images

- Holding someone's warm hand or touching their warm skin
- Putting your hands in warm sand at the beach
- Taking a hot bath, shower, or sitting in a sauna
- Cuddling a baby, warm furry puppy, or kitten
- Holding a warm cup of tea or cocoa
- Holding your hands in front of a fire
- Being wrapped in a warm towel

SURROUND YOURSELF WITH SOOTHING SCENTS

Certain scents are known to have mood enhancing, calming, or stimulating effects. Use an essential oil diffuser and the following essential oils.

SCENT	HELPFUL FOR
Lavender	Anxiety Grief Memory Pain Relief
Chamomile	Anxiety
Jasmine	Anxiety
Ylang Ylang	Memory Trauma Anger
Peppermint	Stimulating
Eucalyptus	Stimulating Focus

LOVING KINDNESS MEDITATION

One of our favorite forms of meditation is called Loving Kindness Meditation (LKM), which is intended to develop feelings of goodwill and warmth toward others. It has been found to quickly increase positive emotions and decrease negative ones, decrease pain and migraine headaches, reduce symptoms of posttraumatic stress disorder, & increase gray matter in the emotional processing areas of the brain, and boost social connectedness.

Exercise: Practice Loving Kindness Meditation.

1. Sit in a comfortable and relaxed position and close your eyes.

2. Take 2-3 deep breaths, taking twice as long to exhale.

3. Let any worries or concerns drift away and feel your breath

moving through the area around your heart.

As you sit, quietly or silently repeat the following or similar phrases:

May I be safe and secure

May I be healthy and strong

May I be happy and purposeful

May I be at peace

Let the intentions expressed in these phrases sink in as you repeat them. Allow the feelings to grow deeper. After a few repetitions, direct the phrases to someone you feel grateful for or someone who has helped you:

May I be safe and secure

May I be healthy and strong

May I be happy and purposeful

May I be at peace

Next, visualize someone you feel neutral about. Choose among people you neither like nor dislike and repeat the phrases.

Next, visualize someone you don't like or with whom you are having a hard time. Kids who are being teased or bullied at school often feel quite empowered when they send love to the people who are making them miserable.

Finally, direct the phrases toward everyone universally.

May I be safe and secure

May I be healthy and strong

May I be happy and purposeful

May I be at peace

You can do this for 10-30 minutes; it's up to you.

GENERALIZED RELAXATION (ESCALATOR)
Step 1-Sit in a comfortable chair with your feet on the floor and your hands in your lap

Step 2 -Pick a spot on a wall that is a little bit above your eye level. Stare at the spot, as you do count slowly to 20. Notice that your eyelids soon begin to feel heavy, as if they want to close. Let them. In fact, even if they don't feel as if they want to close, slowly lower them as you get to 20.

Step 3 - Take the deepest breath you can and very slowly exhale. Repeat three times. With each inhale, imagine taking in peace and calmness, and with each exhale, blow out all of the tension- all the things getting in the way of your relaxing. By this time, you'll notice a calm come over you.

Step 4 _ Tightly as you can, squeeze the muscles in your eyelids. Slowly let the muscles in your eyelids relax. Imagine that relaxation spreading everywhere on your body.

Step 5 -After your body feels relaxed, imagine yourself at the top of an escalator. Step on the escalator and ride down, slowly counting backwards from 10. By the time you reach the bottom, you'll be very relaxed.

Step 6 -Enjoy the relaxation for several moments then get back on the escalator riding up Counting to 10 as you go. When you get to 10, open your eyes, feeling relaxed, refreshed, and wide awake.

Once you've practiced this technique a few times, add the following steps:

1. Choose a haven (instructions below) -a place where you feel comfortable and that you can imagine with all of your senses. Your haven can be any real or imaginary place where you'd like to spend time.

2. After you reach the bottom of the escalator, use all your senses to imagine yourself in your special haven. Stay for several minutes. This is where the fun starts and where your mind becomes ripe for change.

3. Begin to experience yourself- not as you currently are, but as you want to be. Plan on spending at least 20 minutes a day on this refueling, life changing exercise. You'll be amazed at the results.

VISUALIZING YOUR HAVEN

1. Pick a special place that makes you feel calm and relaxed. This place can be real or imagined. If you need some help, look at different pictures of peaceful places to get some ideas (e.g., lakes, oceans, beaches, wooded areas, cabins, camping spots, planets, clouds, etc.).

2. Next, make a mental picture of your special place and keep it in your head. When you feel anxious, imagine yourself in your special place.

- What would you smell?

- What types of sounds would you hear?

- What would you be doing?

- What colors would you see?

- Would it be day or night?

All of these questions will help you visualize your special place.

3. Imagine yourself calm and relaxed in your special place. If it helps, cut out, draw, or print off your picture if you would like something tangible to remind you.

4. Practice visualizing your special place even when you don't feel anxious. Practice at night when you're trying to fall asleep.

CREATE AN EMOTIONAL RESCUE PLAYLIST

Music can soothe, inspire, improve your mood, and help you focus. In his powerful book, *The Secret Language of the Heart*, Barry Goldstein reviews the neuroscience properties of music and finds that it can:

- Stimulate emotional circuits in the brain
- Release oxytocin, the cuddle hormone
- Create peak emotions, which increase the amount of dopamine

Without lyrics (words can be distracting):

- Sonata for Two Pianosin D Major (K. 448) – Mozart
- Clair de Lune – Debussy
- Adagio for Strings – Samuel Barber
- Piano Sonata No. 17 in D Minor ("The Tempest") – Beethoven
- Weightless – Marconi Union

- Flotus – Flying Lotus
- Lost In Thought – Jon Hopkins
- Brain-enhancing music pieces specifically composed to enhance mood, memory,gratitude, creativity, energy, focus, motivation, and inspiration by Barry Goldstein (can be found at BrainMD.com).

With lyrics:
- Good Vibrations – The Beach Boys
- Don't Stop Me Now – Queen
- Uptown Girl – Billy Joel
- Dancing Queen – Abba
- Eye of the Tiger – Survivor
- I'm a Believer – The Monkeys
- Girls Just Wanna Have Fun – Cyndi Lauper
- Livin' on a Prayer – Bon Jovi

MY ONE-PAGE MIRACLE

What do you want for your life? What are you going to do to make it happen? Next to each subheading below, briefly write out what's important to you in that area; write what you want, not what you don't want. Be positive and use the first person.

Write what you want with confidence and the expectation that you will make it happen. After you complete this exercise, put it up where you can see and read it every day.

Health:

_____

_____

Nutrition:

_____

_____

Emotional Health:

_____

_____

Physical Health:

_____

_____

Spiritual Health:

_____

_____

Relationships
Family/Friends:

_____

_____

Work/Education:

_____

_____

Money
Short-term:

_____

_____

Long-term:

_____

_____

8050 Beckett Center Dr., Suite 211, West Chester OH 45069
513.874.5433
www.lifecca.com

WHAT ARE YOUR BARRIERS?

Identify barriers to your success and understand the issues that are preventing you from making the changes you need to in order to achieve your goals. Some common barriers include:

> • *Now knowing motivation – if you don't know your "why," you are less likely to succeed.* • *Never saying, "Then what?" – not thinking about the consequences of your actions.* • *Low blood sugar – skipping meals can lead to indecision and/or poor judgment.* • *Poor sleep – the brain undergoes important processes during sleep; do not skimp!* • *ANTs and "little lies" – believing every stupid thought that enters your head.*

1._____

_____

2._____

_____

3._____

_____

4._____

_____

5._____

_____

Now that you've written out some of your barriers, let's discuss...

8050 Beckett Center Dr., Suite 211, West Chester OH 45069
513.874.5433
www.lifecca.com

ANT THERAPY

CORRECTING THE AUTOMATIC NEGATIVE THOUGHTS THAT STEAL YOUR HAPPINESS AND ROB YOUR JOY

One of the most effective techniques Dr. Amen gives all his patients is called ANT Therapy or learning how to kill the ANTs (automatic negative thoughts). He coined this term in the early '90s after a hard day at the office, during which he had several very difficult sessions that day with patients in crisis. When he got home that evening, he found an ant infestation in his kitchen. It was gross. As he started to clean them up, the acronym came to him. He thought of his patients from that day—like his infested kitchen, his patients' brains were also infested by the negative thoughts that were robbing them of their joy and stealing their happiness.

The next day, he brought a can of ant spray to work as a visual aide and have been working diligently ever since to help his patients eradicate their ANTs.

Here are the "ANT Killing" principles we use to help people feel better fast:

1. Every time you have a thought, your brain releases chemicals.

   That's how our brains work: you have a thought...your brain releases chemicals...an electrical transmission goes across your brain and you become aware of what you're thinking. Thoughts are real and they have a direct impact on how you feel and how you behave.

2. Every time you have a mad thought, an unkind thought, a sad thought, or a cranky thought, your brain releases negative chemicals that make you feel bad.

   Think about the last time you were mad. How did you feel physically? When most people are mad, their muscles get tense, their heart beats faster, their hands start to sweat, and they may even begin to feel a little dizzy. Your body reacts to every negative thought you have.

3. Every time you have a good thought, a happy thought, a hopeful thought, or a kind thought your brain releases chemicals that make your body feel good.

• Think about the last time you had a really happy thought. What did you feel inside your body? When most people are happy their muscles relax and their heartbeat and breathing slow down. Your body also reacts to your good thoughts.

4. Thoughts are very powerful!

• They can make your mind and body feel good or they can make you feel bad. Every cell in your body is affected by every thought you have. That is why when people get emotionally upset they often develop physical symptoms, such as headaches or stomach aches.

5. Thoughts lie; they lie a lot, but it is your unquestioned or uninvestigated thoughts that make you sad, mad, nervous, or out of control.

• Unfortunately, if you never challenge your thoughts, you always "believe them."

The negative thoughts invade your mind like ants at a picnic. One negative thought, like one ant at a picnic, is not a big deal. Two or three negative thoughts, like two or three ants at a picnic, become more irritating. And ten or twenty negative thoughts can cause real problems.

6. You can train your thoughts to be positive and hopeful or you can just allow them to be negative and upset you.

• Once you learn about your thoughts, you can choose to think good thoughts and feel good, or you can choose to think bad thoughts and feel lousy. That's right, it's up to you. Research has shown that positive emotions—especially a sense of awe—can reduce inflammation (which hurts your health). You can learn how to change your thoughts and change the way you feel.

7. Surround yourself with people who provide positive bonding.

• If you spend a lot of time with negative people, their negativity will rub off on you. Attitudes are contagious and can have a hidden influence over your thoughts, moods, and behaviors.

©2016 Daniel G. Amen, M.D.

Nine Different Types of ANTs (or ways we distort reality to make it worse than it really is):

• ANT 1 – "Always/never thinking" or "all or nothing" thinking in words like always, never, no one, everyone, every time,everything (thoughts that things are all good or all bad).

• ANT 2 – Focusing on the negative-your thoughts reflect only the bad in a situation or ignore any of the good. Look for things to be glad about in any situation.

• ANT 3 – Fortune telling-this is where you predict the worst possible outcome to a situation with little or no evidence for it. When you predict bad things, you help make them happen.

• ANT 4 – Mind reading-happens when you believe that you know what other people are thinking even when they haven't told you.

• ANT 5 – Thinking with your feelings-occurs when you believe your negative feelings without ever questioning them. Feelings are very complex and often based on powerful memories from the past. Feelings can lie or not be about the truth. They are just feelings. Look for evidence behind those feelings. Are the feelings based on events in the past.

• ANT 6 – Guilt beating-guilt is not a helpful emotion, especially for the deep limbic system. Guilt often causes you to do things you don't want to do. Words like should, must, ought, or have to. Whenever we think we must do something, no matter what it is, we often don't want to do it. Replace with what I want to.

• ANT 7 – Labeling-whenever you attach a negative label to yourself or to someone else, you stop your ability to take a clear look at the situation (e.g., jerk, arrogant...) negative labels are harmful.

• ANT 8 – Personalizing-occurs when you invest in innocuous events with personal meaning (my boss didn't talk to me this morning, she must be mad at me...) You never fully know why people do what they do. Try not to personalize the behavior of others.

• ANT 9 – Blaming-very harmful. When you blame something or someone else for the problems in your life, you become a passive victim of circumstances and you make it very difficult to do anything to change your situation.

BITTER TO BETTER

ANT KILLING EXERCISE:
Whenever you feel sad, mad, nervous, or out of control, write down your automatic negative thoughts, label them, then "kill" them by talking back to them.

Here are some ANT Killing examples:

ANT Species of ANT Kill the ANT

My wife never listens to me. Always Thinking That's just not true. She often listens to me. Today she is just distracted.

My boss doesn't like me. Mind Reading I don't know that for sure. Maybe she's just having a bad day. I need to talk to her.

I'm a failure. Labeling Sometimes I fail, but many times I succeed

It's my husband's fault. Blame I will look at my part of the problem and look for ways to make it better.

Your thoughts matter. Learn to kill the ANTs and train your thoughts to be positive—it will benefit your mind, mood, and body.

KILL THE ANTS WORKSHEET: Use the information below to create a worksheet to help you get control of your automatic negative thoughts.

When you notice an ANT:

    1. Write it down.

    2. Identify the type of ANT it is.

    3. Kill the ANT by talking back to it - challenge the thought!

    4. Ask yourself the seven questions that follow.

1. What's your ANT?

_____

_____

2. What type of ANT is it? _____

_____

3. Kill the ANT by talking back to it:

4. The Seven Questions

1. Is it true?_____

2. Is it absolutely true with 100% certainty? _____

3. How do I feel when I believe this thought? _____

_____

_____

4. How would I feel or who would I be if I couldn't have this thought?

_____

_____

5. How do you treat yourself or others when you have this thought?

_____

_____

6. Can you see a good reason to hold onto this thought?

_____

_____

7. (Turn the thought around to the exact opposite, then ask) Is the opposite of the thought true or even truer than the original thought? Give 3 true examples of the opposite thought.

_____

_____

_____

AMEN CLINICS SUGGESTED BLOOD PANEL

Most PCPs do not administer the Food sensitivity test and the DUTCH Test; and may not administer the Immunity/infection test. You may have to find a Functional/Integrative Doctor to administer those.

The immunity/infection test is normally run if other medications, prior treatment, or diet have not made a difference.

The difference between the DUTCH test and the Cortisol, DHEA, hormone blood test done by PCPs is the DUTCH test is a dried urine test administered 5x over a 24-hour period. You can watch the explanation video here: https://dutchtest.com/info-dutch-complete/

AMEN CLINICS SUGGESTED BLOOD PANEL:
I do recommend that all my clients get the following blood tests (below) to rule out any underlying conditions. Often, the doctors say they "do not normally run these tests" so you will need to be your own advocate. It's better to rule out any medical conditions at the beginning.

1. **Food SENSITIVITY** –NOT FOOD ALLERGY (May need to go to a Functional/Integrative Medical Doctor).

2. **General CBC (Complete Blood Count w/differential)** – this blood test checks the health of your blood, including red and white blood cell counts. People with low blood count (anemia) can feel anxious and tired and may overeat as a way to medicate themselves. A high level of white blood cells may indicate infection.

3. **Blood Pressure** – High or too low of blood pressure=low blood flow to brain.

Optimal: Systolic 90-120, Diastolic 60-80

Stage 1 Hypertension: Systolic 130-139, Diastolic 80-89

Stage 2 Hypertension: Systolic ≥ 140, Diastolic ≥ 90

Hypotension (too low can also be a problem): Systolic < 90, Diastolic < 60

4. **Hemoglobin A1C (HbA1C) & Fasting Insulin**
This test shows your average blood sugar levels over the past 2-3 months and is used to diagnose diabetes and prediabetes.

Normal results for someone without diabetes: 4% - 5.6%

Optimal: < 5.3%

Pre-diabetes: 5.7% - 6.4%

5. Lipid panel & particle size
Make sure your doctor checks total cholesterol level as well as HDL (good cholesterol), LDL (bad cholesterol), and triglycerides(a form of fat).

Normal levels are:
Total cholesterol: 135 - 200 mg/dL

Optimal: 160-200 mg/dL (Note: levels below 160 have been associated with ADD, depression, suicide,& homicide)

HDL: >/= 60 mg/dL

LDL: <100 mg/dL

Triglycerides: <100 mg/dL

6. Ferritin – A measure of iron stores, a number that increases with inflammation and insulin resistance. You don't want ferritin levels that are too low, as this is associated with anemia, insomnia, restless leg syndrome, ADD, depression, and low motivation (not able to produce enough dopamine) and energy. High iron stores have been associated with stiffer blood vessels and vascular disease.

Optimal: 50 - 100 ng/mL

7. Free/total testosterone (OR SEE DUTCH Test) – Low levels of testosterone, for men or women, are associated with low energy, heart disease, obesity, depression, and Alzheimer's disease. Testosterone is the motivation hormone in males. Too low=low to no motivation.

Normal levels:
Men
Total Testosterone: 280-800 ng/dL Optimal: 500 - 800 ng/dL
Free Testosterone: 7.2-24 picogram (pg)/mL Optimal: 12 - 24 pg/mL

Women
Total Testosterone: 6-82 ng/dL Optimal: 40 - 82 ng/dL
Free Testosterone: 0.0-2.2 pg/mL Optimal: 1.0 - 2.2 pg/m

8. DHEA – A DHEAS test is useful in determining whether the adrenal glands are working properly.

Typical Normal for Females	*Typical Normal for Males*
Ages 18-19 | 145-395 mcg/dL	Ages 18-19 | 108-441 mcg/dL
Ages 20-29 | 65-380 mcg/dL	Ages 20-29 | 280-640 mcg/dL
Ages 30-39 | 45-270 mcg/dL	Ages 30-39 | 120-520 mcg/dL
Ages 40-49 | 32-240 mcg/dL	Ages 40-49 | 95-530 mcg/dL
Ages 50-59 | 26-200 mcg/dL	Ages 50-59 | 70-310 mcg/dL
Ages 60-69 | 13-130 mcg/dL	Ages 60-69 | 42-290 mcg/dL
Ages 70+ | 17-90 mcg/dL	Ages 70+ | 28-175 mcg/dL

9. CORTISOL (OR SEE DUTCH TEST)

Optimal: 11-14 ug/dL

10. DUTCH TEST (COMPLETE – Women, PLUS-Men) (https://dutchtest.com/dutch-testing/)

This test looks at sex hormones and their metabolites, the overall diurnal pattern of free cortisol, and the total and distribution of cortisol metabolites in addition to OATs which provide insight into nutritional deficiencies, oxidative stress, gut dysbiosis, melatonin, neuroinflammation and more.

Healthcare providers can use this valuable tool to optimize hormone health and address hormone related symptoms such as fatigue, weight gain, hair loss, and mood swings.

11. C-reactive protein – This is a measure of inflammation, which is associated with several medical conditions. Fat cells produce chemicals that increase inflammation. This is the best test for inflammation. It measures the general level of inflammation but does not tell you where it is from. The most common reason for an elevated C-reactive protein is metabolic syndrome or insulin resistance. The second most common is some sort of reaction to food—either a sensitivity, a true allergy, or an autoimmune reaction as occurs with gluten. It can also indicate hidden infections.

Healthy range: 0.0 - 1.0 mg/dL

12. Homocysteine – is an amino acid that, when elevated, is associated with inflammation, atherosclerosis, and an increased risk of heart attack, stroke, blood clots, and possibly Alzheimer's disease. Homocysteine is a sensitive marker for folate deficiency.

Healthy range: <8 micromoles/liter

13. Folate – aids in the production of DNA and other genetic material. It is required for the healthy regulation of our genes and is especially important when cells and tissues are growing rapidly, such as an infancy, adolescence, and in pregnancy. Folate works together with vitamin B6 and B12 and other nutrients to control blood levels of homocysteine. It is common to have low levels of folate as a result of alcoholism, inflammatory bowel disease, celiac disease, and taking certain medications.

Normal: 2-20 ng/mL

Optimal: >3 ng/mL

14. Vitamin B12

Healthy range: 211-946 pg/mL

15. Magnesium

16. Thyroid-TSH, Free T3, Free T4, and thyroid antibodies – Having low thyroid levels decreases overall brain activity, which can impair your thinking, judgment, and self-control, and make it very hard for you to lose weight. There is no one perfect way, no one symptom or test result, that will properly diagnose low thyroid function or hypothyroidism. The key is to look at symptoms and blood tests, and then decide.

TSI: 0.00-0.55 IU/L

TSH Healthy range: 0.4 - 3.0 mIU/L or 1.8-3.0 ULU/mL

TT4: 6.0-12.0 UD/GL

TT3: 100-180 ng/dL

Free T3 Healthy range: 3.0-4.0 pg/ml

T3 Uptake: 28.0%-38.0%

Reverse T3: 9-24 ng/dL

Free T4 Healthy range: 1.0-1.80 ng/dl

TPO Antibody: 0-34 iu/mL

Thyroglobulin Antibody: 0.0-0.9 iu/mL

17. 25-hydroxy Vitamin D levels

Low levels of vitamin D have been associated with obesity, depression, cognitive impairment, heart disease, and many other diseases. Have your physician check your 25-hydroxy vitamin D level, and if it is low, get more sunshine and/or take a vitamin D3 supplement.

Low: < 30 nanograms/deciliter

Optimal: between 50 - 100 ng/dl

18. AA/EPA ratio (Ratio between Omega 6 (unhealthy type) & Omega 3 (healthy type))

Optimal: <3
>3 associated with inflammation and higher levels associated with depression.

19. General Metabolic Panel – The organs that detoxify your body—especially the liver, kidneys, and skin—need to be supported to do their job. The tests below will tell you how these organs are coping with your body's toxic load. Liver Function

- ALT (SGPT): Normal range: 7 - 56 units per liter (U/L)
- AST (SGOT): Normal range: 5 - 40 U/L
- Bilirubin: Normal range: 0.2 - 1.2 mg/dL
- Zinc: Normal range: 60 - 110 mcg/dL (low zinc will limit detoxification in the liver)

Kidney Function

- BUN: Normal range: 7 - 20 mg/dL
- Creatinine: Normal range: 0.5 - 1.2 mg/dL

20. Immunity or Infectious Disease Tests if you have a history of allergies, rashes, or repeated infections, it could indicate an immune system vulnerability.

Testing for Mold
•TGF beta-1: Normal level: below 2,380; 0 is optimal. Mold exposure can raise this to more than 15,000

Real Time Labs mycotoxin test (http://www.realtimelab.com/home): for mold tests of human & environmental samples

Testing for Heavy Metals
Hair sample and urinary "challenge" tests are common

Erythrocyte Sedimentation Rate (ESR) – This common test is a nonspecific measure of inflammation, which is high in autoimmune disorders.

Antinuclear antibodies (ANA) – the immune system normally makes antibodies to help fight infection, but antinuclear antibodies often attack the body's own tissues. Test results are often high in autoimmune disorders.

Rheumatoid factor (Rh) – Rh it is an antibody that is measurable in the blood. It can bind to other antibodies and cause problems.

Screening for common infections:
• Borrelia burgdorferi (the spirochete that causes Lyme disease)

• Toxoplasma gondii (transmitted through Cats/Cat litter)

• Epstein Barr virus

• Streptococcus

• Cytomegalovirus

• Helicobacter pylori

• Herpes simplex one and two

• Syphilis

• Chlamydophila pneumoniae

• HIV/AIDS

21. **Genetic-APOE4 Gene Type ("Alzheimer Gene")** – for children if they are going to play sports where head injury is a risk.

APPENDIX II

APPENDIX II

Meet Debbie Day, a lifelong friend, who has served as editor for all of my published books. We have worked together in both Christian and public schools and in multiple programs for marginalized students. We both see reading and writing as important skills, as well as good tools for therapy, for reflection, and for introspection. From the inception of a manuscript through the final editing process, Debbie has been a great help with clarifications, perspectives, and detailed readings of each version of every book. Recently, Debbie has begun writing memoirs about her pastor father and life as a PK (preacher's kid). She shared this beautiful piece about traditions, legacies, and family dynamics. I asked for her permission to share this nostalgic piece so that more readers can appreciate this wonderful author who makes my life and my books so much better because of her faithfulness to God and her wonderful sense of humor. Enjoy!

Debbie Day with grandchildren Nora, Jay, and Ralphie.

FRIED CHICKEN LOVE

The last time my mom fried chicken for us, we didn't know it was the last time. The small apartment kitchen was a wreck as usual whenever and wherever she cooked. Flour everywhere, down her shirt, on the floor getting tracked by her bare feet as she sprinted from the refrigerator to the counter to the stove and back again. There was oil splattered all over the stovetop. The potatoes were bubbling hard, rocking to their own beat as they splashed starchy water all around. The biscuits were lined up on the cooking sheet that was blackened and beaten from years of use and abuse, waiting to be shoved into the oven at the last minute to ensure piping hot golden flakiness when we sat down to eat. The tea bags had already been boiled and poured into the plastic pitcher that had several melted spots on the handle from close calls with hot burners. With water and sugar added, sweet tea would soon be concocted. The meal would be complete with the addition of the shoepeg corn like Grandma Ellis always made, but this time it was in a plastic pouch in the microwave. The table had been set hours before with the "good" dishes and silverware alongside the peach colored linen napkins with the fancy bamboo napkin rings.

She had just moved into her new apartment that my sister had helped her get all fixed up. She helped her get a new sofa and a smaller, but just as lovely as the one before, dining room set. The apartment was across town from where I was living and with going back to full time teaching and the busyness of the kids playing sports, I didn't have a lot of time to spend with Mom at her new place. She used the best bait she knew of to get us to visit her, by offering to fix us her famous fried chicken dinner. From the kitchen chaos, came the beautiful golden brown chicken cut into small, crispy pieces like she always did. She first started cutting up the chicken that way to make enough to go around for our family, when it became four kids plus Mama and Daddy. We all prefer the small pieces now - all white meat of course, a choice we did not have when it came from a whole chicken.

My first memory of chickens is from when we lived in Kentucky and raised them. I hated them. They were mean. When I walked out in the yard where they wandered freely to give them a treat of pieces of bread, one would invariably run up and grab the piece of bread out of my hand before I could break it up and scatter it around. It always startled me; I couldn't have been more than four years old, and it alway made me mad. Hateful chickens! When it was time to kill one for cooking, I watched my mom wring the neck and then pour scalding water on it to pluck the feathers. I don't think I watched with delightful revenge in my eyes. I hope not. The smell of those wet feathers was not pleasant, but we suffered the process for the joy that we knew was to come.

I guess it was Daddy's love for chicken that started the tradition of the delicious special meals. Daddy was the pastor of a small Kentucky church and the congregation knew how much he loved chicken, so when families invited us to their homes for meals, it was often chicken. When a visiting evangelist came to town to preach a week, sometimes ten day revival, the custom was to feed the evangelist and pastor's family at a different home each day. One revival, we ate both lunch and dinner each day. Since my sister was in school, and I was not, I was given both the legs. At the end of the week, Mama counted up that I had eaten twenty chicken legs!

Later, when we moved to Ohio and my brothers came along, and mine and my sister's palates were more sophisticated, we got sweet, tender pieces of white meat breast, and the boys got the legs. One Sunday, a rare one when we weren't invited to someone's home, Mama labored quickly and hard to get fried chicken ready after church. Again, Daddy being the pastor, we often did not get home immediately after the service, as he had to counsel or just socialize with people after church. We were all starving and wanting Sunday dinner as soon as Mama could throw it together. That she could do, and I'm sure that's what got her in the habit of being so messy when she cooked. That Sunday, while waiting to be called in to eat, I went out in the backyard to play baseball with Stevie, my brother closest in age to me, but still five years younger. We weren't really playing a game; what we usually did was play coach and player. Of course, I was the coach, and I would throw and hit balls at Stevie shouting instructions on how to field a grounder playing the short hop or how to catch a fly ball making sure to use two hands. Then I would pitch to him and coach him on how to hit. This day, I decided to teach him how to hit a curveball. The only problem was that I didn't know how to throw a curveball. I rocked back on the board we used for a pitching rubber, and shouted, "Watch this curveball!" The ball slipped from my fingers before I was ready to let go of it and went sailing toward the house crashing through the kitchen window and scattering glass all over the plate of chicken Mama had just placed on the table. Everyone shouted and groaned, and I think Mama cried. I know I did because Daddy chastened me harshly for doing such a "stupid thing"! I'm telling the truth, I'm pretty sure we brushed off the glass and ate the chicken anyway. We had to!

That last fried chicken dinner my mom cooked was every bit as good as any she had ever made. After dinner, my sister and I started cleaning up and reminiscing about how when we were growing up, we were assigned to doing the dishes after every supper my mom cooked. We would try to sneak out after eating to get in a few more minutes of play before it got dark, but we were always hollered back into the kitchen. We took turns washing or drying, but there always seemed to be a debate over whose turn it actually was to wash, since that was the job we both hated. I'm not sure why it was so hard to keep track, since it was only the two of us, but I think we tried to argue that if we happened to eat somewhere else the day before, that counted as our turn. Our delay tactics did not work to our advantage, as we ended up still in the kitchen long after suppertime.

That last fried chicken dinner my mom cooked, Luke, my son, was 16 by then and he brought his new girlfriend, Trisha, (now wife and mother of two of my grandchildren) along for the feast. After dinner, Luke and Trisha and my daughter, Whitney (by the way is now the mother of my other grandchild, I'd be remiss not to mention), wanted to go to a store called "Steve and Barry's" that sold athletic clothes and jackets. The store was very popular for the short time it lasted because the prices were ridiculously low and the styles were pretty much up to date. My sister volunteered to drive and I stayed back with Mom. When they got back they were all laughing, and I demanded to know what was so funny. They said one of the clerks at the store said to another one, "Do you smell fried chicken? For some reason it smells like fried chicken in here." We all not only had the taste of the delicious fried chicken, but we came away with that mouth watering aroma as well.

BITTER TO BETTER

It was just a short while after this night that Mom began showing signs of dementia. At first, it seemed to be harmless forgetfulness or confusion, but it quickly became more serious. She wasn't able to stay in her apartment long, and eventually had to go to assisted living and then to a full care facility. We didn't know that was the last time she would fry chicken for us, but we'll never forget it.

I still fry chicken for my family for birthdays or other occasions, when I get the chance. This past December twenty years later, Luke requested fried chicken for his birthday dinner. Whitney just recently fried chicken for her husband at their new place in California. She called me as she was cooking to ask my advice on how to get the outside crispy and tender and juicy on the inside like Grandma always did. She marveled at the fact that her husband had never had a home cooked fried chicken dinner. She reported later that the meal turned out perfectly and he loved the chicken. The legacy continues: fried chicken love.